Language Handbook

Grade 1

Printed in the United States of America

ISBN 0-15-325063-1

11 12 073 08 07 06 05

Orlando Boston Dallas Chicago San Diego

Visita *The Learning Site*
www.harcourtschool.com

Contents

WRITING

GRAMMAR, USAGE, AND MECHANICS

Table of Contents

Dear Student,

The Language Handbook will help you speak and write better. It will help you choose the right words to tell about something. Inside are many ideas for writing, too. We hope you have fun learning about your language.

Sincerely,

The Authors

Writing

The Writing Process

A story or a poem is easy to write when you have a plan. First, think about what you want to write, who you are writing for, and why you are writing. Then use these five steps to plan your writing.

PREWRITING

Make a list of ideas to write about. Draw a picture or make a chart of the idea you choose.

DRAFTING

Write about your prewriting idea.
Do not worry about making a mistake.

RESPONDING AND REVISING

Meet with a partner to talk about your draft.
Think about any changes you want to make.

PROOFREADING

Reread or read aloud your revised draft.
Fix any mistakes you find.

PUBLISHING

Think about how you want to share your work.

Name ____________________

Sentences About a Picture

When you draw a picture, you can write about it. Your sentences should answer the questions **Who?** **What?** **Where?** and **When?**

1. **Draw your picture.**
2. **Think about what you want to write.**
3. **Answer the questions Who? What? Where? and When?**

MODEL: SENTENCES ABOUT A PICTURE

The cat is stuck in a tree. We cannot get her down. My sister climbs a tall ladder. She saves the cat!

Name ____________________

Story About You

A **story about you** is one kind of story you can write. In a story about you, you tell about something that you did.

1. **Think about things you have done. Choose one thing to write about.**
2. **Write your story. Tell in order what you did.**
3. **Use the words I and me.**

MODEL: STORY ABOUT YOU

First, I went to the block corner. Next, I built a tall wall. Then Jessie helped me make it into a castle. We showed our castle to everyone in our class.

Name ______________________________

Poem

You can write a **poem**. Some poems have rhyming words. Rhyming words are words that end with the same sounds.

1. **Choose something to write about.**
2. **Think of rhyming words or other words to use.**
3. **Write your poem.**

MODEL: POEM

Elephants are big.
Elephants are gray.
I wish I could play
With an elephant today!

Name ______________________________

Friendly Letter

You can write a **friendly letter** to someone you know. In it, you tell something about yourself. A friendly letter has five parts.

1. **Think about things to tell about yourself. Choose one idea.**
2. **Write a letter to your friend.**
3. **Use the five parts that are shown by the arrows.**

MODEL: FRIENDLY LETTER

April 17, 200_ ←

→ Dear Sarah,

→ Today I had my first soccer game. I tried to kick the ball. I missed two times. Then I kicked the ball really hard. It went into the goal! We lost, but we had fun!

Your friend, ←

Kim ←

Name ________________________________

Description

When you write a **description**, you tell about something. You use words that tell how the thing looks, sounds, tastes, smells, or feels.

1. **Think about things you have seen. Choose one to write about.**
2. **Write a description. Tell what the thing was like.**
3. **Use words that tell how it looked, sounded, tasted, smelled, or felt.**

MODEL: DESCRIPTION

The Farm

Our class went to a farm. We saw lots of cows. They were big and gentle. The farmers gave us ice cream they made on the farm. It was cold and sweet and good!

Name ______________________________

Story

You can write a **story** about someone or something. A story tells what happens to a person, animal, or thing.

1. **Think of ideas for a story. Choose one to write about.**
2. **Write your story. Tell who it is about and what happens.**
3. **Write a title for your story.**

MODEL: STORY

Sam's New Sled

Sam had a new sled, but there was no snow. He waited and waited. At last, he put his sled away. In the morning Sam had a big surprise. It was snowing!

Name ____________________________________

Riddle

A **riddle** is a word puzzle. You write clues in a riddle. Your friends guess what the riddle is about.

1. **Think of things you can write riddles about. Choose one.**
2. **Write your clues. Ask a question at the end.**
3. **Turn your paper around and write the answer.**

MODEL: RIDDLE

I am a bug.
I am small and round.
I am red with black spots.
I do not bite.
What am I?

(a ladybug)

Name ____________________

Book Report

A **book report** tells about a book you have read.

1. **Write the name of the book. Underline it.**
2. **Write the author's name.**
3. **Tell who or what the book is about. Tell your favorite part.**

MODEL: BOOK REPORT

<u>A Pet for Maria</u>

by Kate McGovern

This book is about Maria. She wants a pet. First, she asks her parents for a horse. Next, she asks for a dog. Then she asks for a cat. My favorite part is when Maria and her parents go to buy her new pet, a goldfish.

Name ____________________

How-To Sentences

How-to sentences tell how to do or make something. When you write about how to do something, you tell the steps in order.

1. **Think about things you know how to do. Choose one to write about.**
2. **Write how to do that thing. Tell the steps in the right order.**
3. **Use order words like first and last.**

MODEL: HOW-TO SENTENCES

Here's how to wash a dog. First, fill a tub with soap and water. Next, put the dog in the tub and wash him. Then, rinse the dog off with clean water. Last, use a towel to dry the dog.

Name ____________________

Scene

A scene is one part of a story or play. When you write a scene, you tell who is speaking. Then you write the words that character says.

1. **Think about characters. Choose some to write about.**
2. **Think about what the characters do and say.**
3. **Write the scene. Use the exact words the characters say.**

MODEL: SCENE

Rabbit: Sheep, do you want to play a game?
Sheep: No thanks, Rabbit. I'm working in my garden.
Rabbit: May I help?
Sheep: Sure. Here are some seeds.

Grammar, Usage, and Mechanics

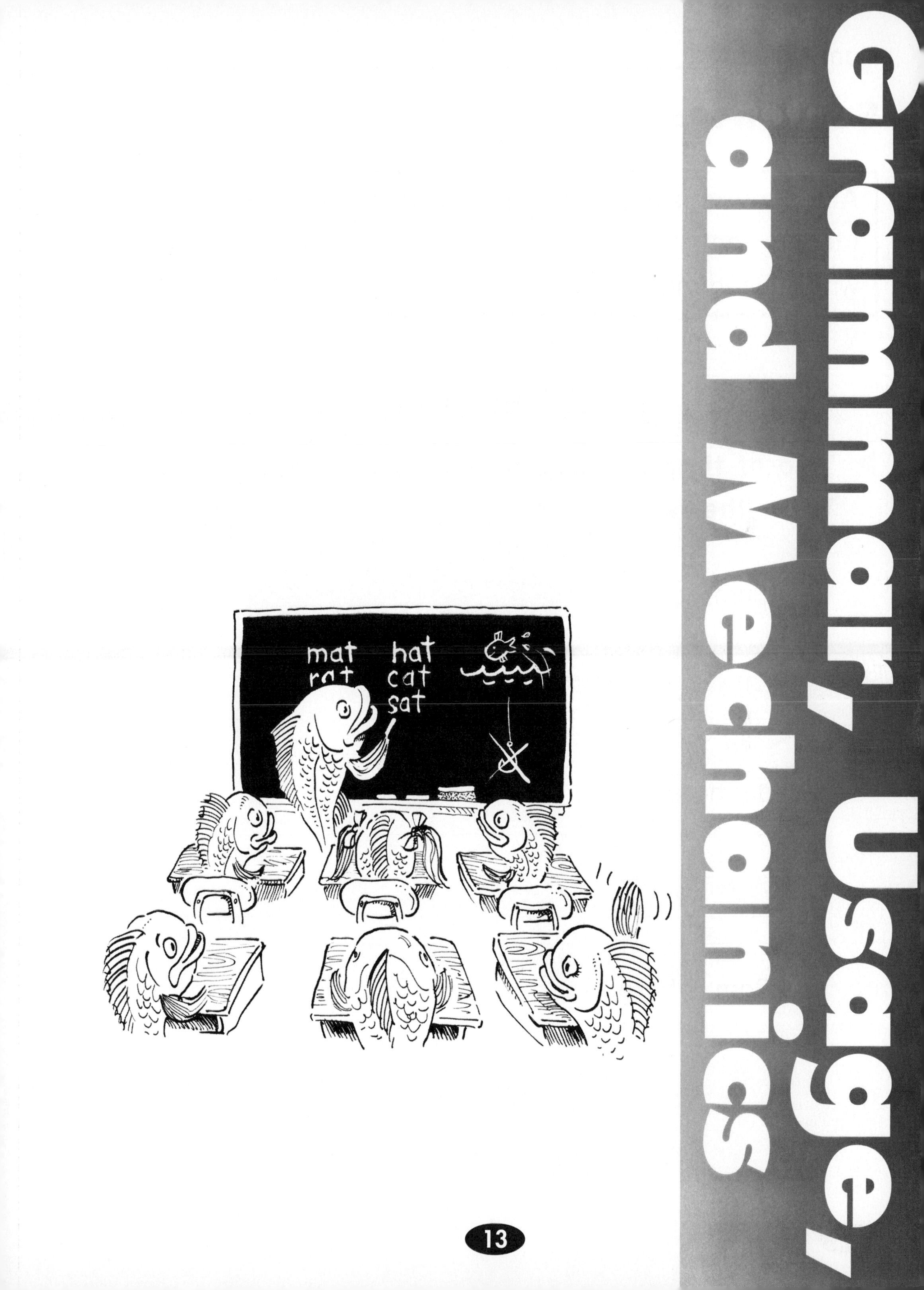

Name ______________________________

Sentences

A **sentence** is a group of words. It tells a complete idea. A sentence begins with a capital letter. It ends with an end mark.

A cat sat.

▶ **Two of these groups of words are sentences. Write the two sentences.**

1. I am Sam.

2. am here

3. Sam is here.

SCHOOL-HOME CONNECTION
Ask your child to say two complete sentences.

Name ______________________________

Sentences

▶ **Circle the sentence under each picture.**

I am Sam.

am Sam

Sam

Sam sat.

A cat sat.

a cat

▶ **Write the sentences you circled.**

1. ______________________________

2. ______________________________

3. ______________________________

SCHOOL-HOME CONNECTION
Have your child read the sentences.

Name ___________________________

Sentences

▶ **Read each group of words. Write the one that is a sentence.**

1. I am a cat. a cat

____

2. I am here. am here

____

3. at me Look at me!

____

4. a mat Here is a mat.

____

SCHOOL-HOME CONNECTION
Ask your child to tell why one group of words in each item is not a sentence.

Name ____________________

Sentences

▶ **Circle each group of words that is a sentence.**

1. am Sam
2. that mat
3. I am here.
4. Sam sat here.
5. at a mat
6. I am Sam.
7. sat at a
8. Sam is a cat.

▶ **Write the sentence that tells about the picture.**

9. ____________________

SCHOOL-HOME CONNECTION
Ask your child to tell how each uncircled group of words could be turned into a sentence.

Name ______________________________

Word Order

Words in a sentence are in order. The words must be in order to make sense.

Matt has cookies.

▶ **Circle the sentence that is in order. Write the other words in order to make sentences.**

1. sat. Pam

____

2. Pam has a cat.

____

3. the cat. I look at

____

SCHOOL-HOME CONNECTION
Say some words that are in order and some that are not. Ask your child to tell which are sentences.

Name ________________________________

Word Order

▶ **Write each group of words correctly to make a sentence.**

1. sat. The cat

____

2. a hat. Pam has

____

3. look good. The cookies

____

4. I the cat. pat

____

SCHOOL-HOME CONNECTION
Ask your child to tell how he or she knew each item was not in correct word order.

Name ______________________________

Word Order

▶ **Draw a line under the sentence that tells about the picture. Then write the sentence.**

1. I tap the map.

tap I the map.

____

2. cap. a has Pat

Pat has a cap.

____

3. pat Sam. I

I pat Sam.

____

SCHOOL-HOME CONNECTION
Ask your child to tell why he or she underlined each item.

Name ___________________________

Word Order

▶ **Underline each group of words that is a sentence.**

1. Matt looks at the cat.

2. is big. The cat

3. The cat sat.

4. Matt pats the cat.

5. a cat. Matt has

▶ **Now turn the other groups of words into sentences. Use correct word order.**

6. ___________________________

7. ___________________________

SCHOOL-HOME CONNECTION
Say words that are not in correct word order. Ask your child to say them in correct word order to make a sentence.

Name ______________________________

Telling Sentences

A **telling sentence** tells about something or someone. It begins with a capital letter. It usually ends with a **period (.)**. A telling sentence that shows strong feeling may end with an **exclamation point (!)**.

The cat sat on the mat.
Sam is mad!

▶ **Write these telling sentences correctly.**

1. Sam has a cap

____

2. a cat is on the cap

____

SCHOOL-HOME CONNECTION
Ask your child to tell what a telling sentence should begin and end with.

Name ______________________________

Telling Sentences

▶ **Circle each telling sentence that is written correctly.**

1. Tim pats his cat.
2. the cat sees the dog
3. I am mad!
4. Pat has a red hat.
5. this map is big

▶ **Now write the other sentences correctly.**

6. ______________________________

7. ______________________________

SCHOOL-HOME CONNECTION
Ask your child to tell how he or she changed each noncircled item to write it correctly.

Name ____________________

Telling Sentences

▶ **Write the first word of each sentence the correct way. Put a . or a ! at the end.**

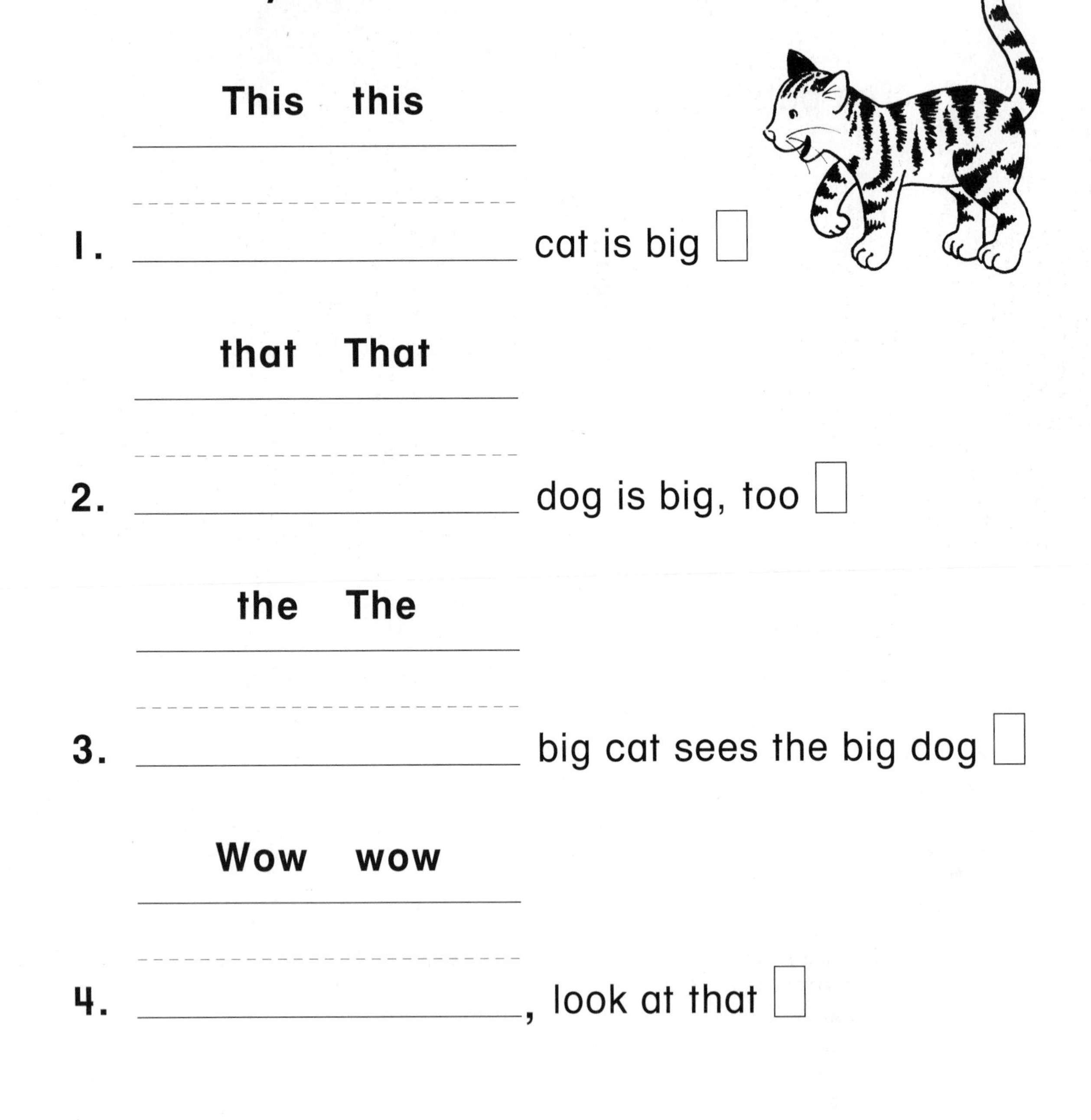

This this

1. ____________ cat is big ☐

that That

2. ____________ dog is big, too ☐

the The

3. ____________ big cat sees the big dog ☐

Wow wow

4. ____________, look at that ☐

SCHOOL-HOME CONNECTION
Ask your child to tell how he or she knew which way to write the word to begin each sentence.

Name ______________________________

Telling Sentences

▶ **Write telling sentences. Use the words in the boxes. Begin and end each telling sentence correctly.**

the look cookies good	the cookies I pass

big a cookie dad has

1. ______________________________

2. ______________________________

3. ______________________________

SCHOOL-HOME CONNECTION
Ask your child to tell how he or she changed each group of words to turn it into a telling sentence.

Name ______________________________

Asking Sentences

An **asking sentence** asks about something or someone. It begins with a capital letter. It ends with a **question mark (?)**.

Is my cat here?

▶ **Two of these sentences are asking sentences. Write the asking sentences correctly.**

1. where is my bike

____

2. my dad had a red hat

____

3. what is in your hand

____

Harcourt

SCHOOL-HOME CONNECTION
Ask your child to tell which sentence is not an asking sentence and why.

Name ______________________________

Asking Sentences

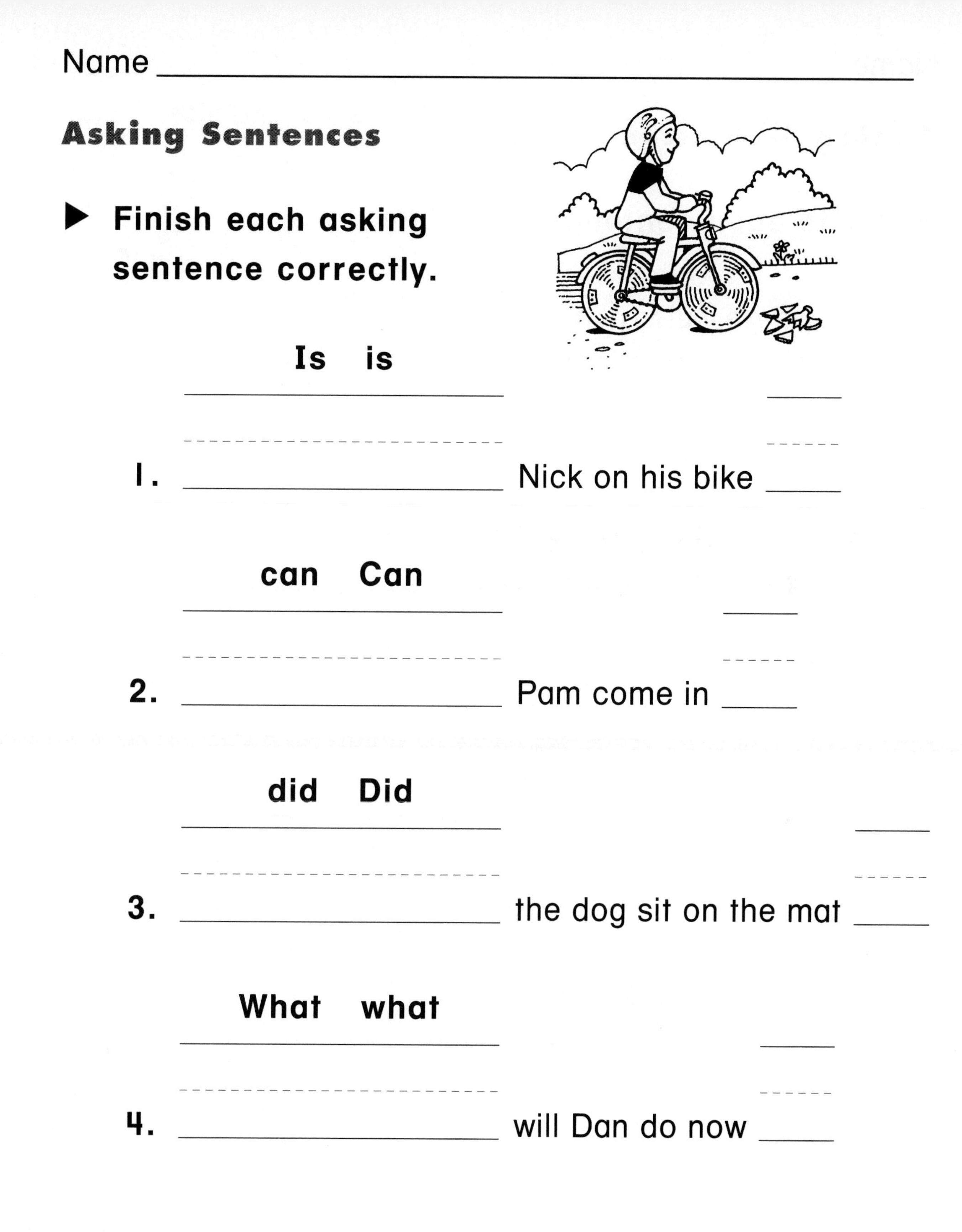

▶ **Finish each asking sentence correctly.**

Is is

1. ____________ Nick on his bike ____

can Can

2. ____________ Pam come in ____

did Did

3. ____________ the dog sit on the mat ____

What what

4. ____________ will Dan do now ____

SCHOOL-HOME CONNECTION
Say a telling sentence and an asking sentence. Have your child tell which one is an asking sentence.

Name ______________________

Asking Sentences

▶ **Write each sentence correctly.**

1. where will you hit it

2. is that apple for me

3. can your dog meow

4. did you pack a snack

SCHOOL-HOME CONNECTION
Say a telling sentence. Ask your child to turn it into an asking sentence.

Name ____________________

Asking Sentences

▶ **Write each sentence from the picture correctly.**

can I come too

did you look at the map

did you pack a snack

1. ____________________

2. ____________________

3. ____________________

SCHOOL-HOME CONNECTION
Have your child say two new asking sentences.

Name ______________________________

Naming Parts of Sentences

A sentence has a **naming part.** The naming part tells who or what the sentence is about.

The apples are red.

▶ **Write the naming part of each sentence.**

1. The cat is big. ______________________

2. The hats are tan. ______________________

3. The man is tall. ______________________

4. Sal is not here. ______________________

SCHOOL-HOME CONNECTION
Ask your child to say a different naming part for each sentence.

Name ______________________________

Naming Parts of Sentences

▶ **Circle the naming part of each sentence. Then write the naming part.**

1. Mack sits down.

2. Pam can kick.

3. A surprise comes to Mack.

4. Two pals can kick.

SCHOOL-HOME CONNECTION
Say a sentence. Ask your child to identify the naming part.

Name ____________________

Naming Parts of Sentences

▶ **Write the correct naming part in each sentence. Use the words in the boxes.**

The pals	The cat
The apple	

1. ____________________ is red.

2. ____________________ see the cat.

3. ____________________ has a nap.

SCHOOL-HOME CONNECTION
Ask your child to use each naming part in a new sentence.

Name ____________________

Naming Parts of Sentences

▶ **Look at each picture. Write the correct naming part for each sentence.**

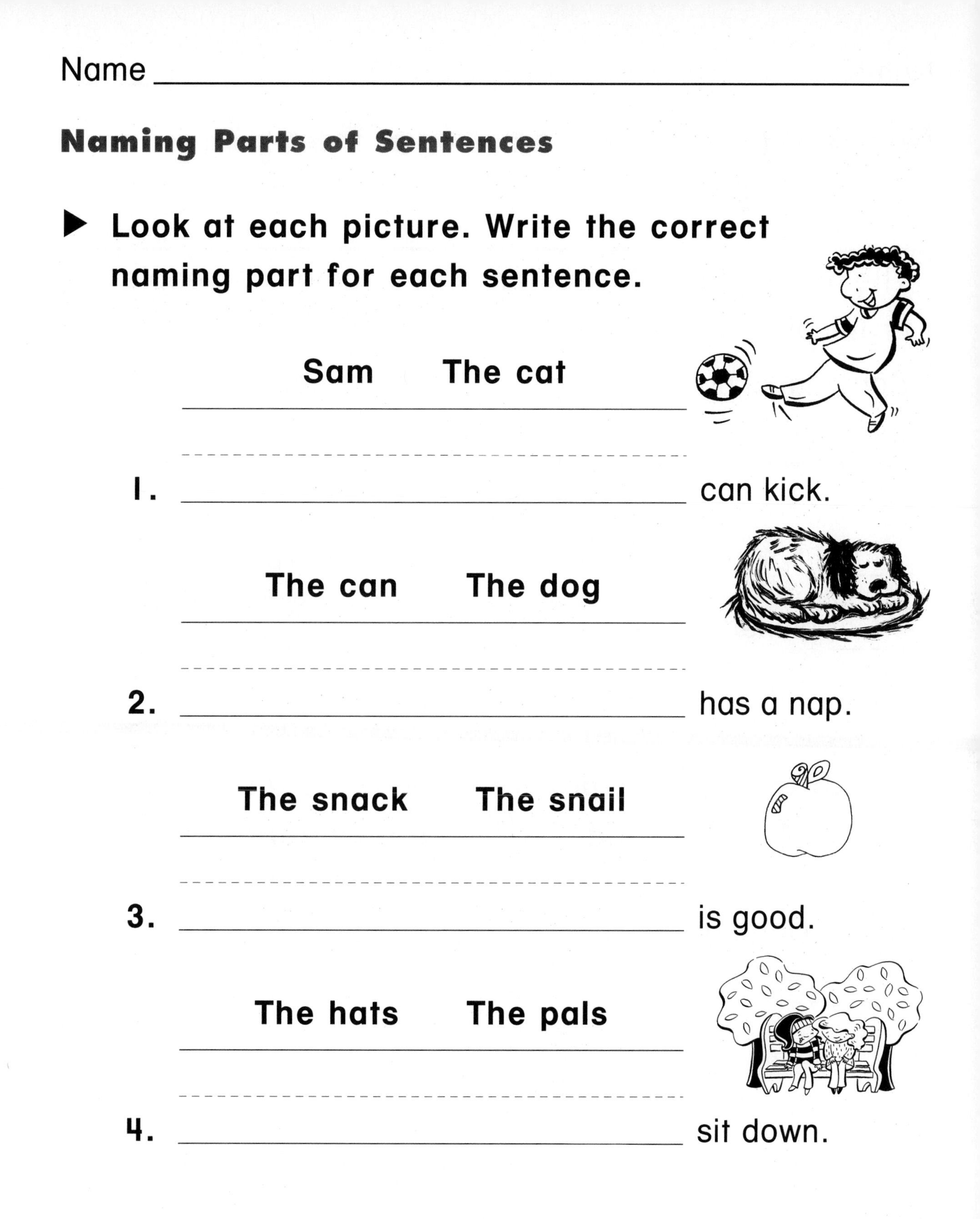

Sam **The cat**

1. ____________________ can kick.

The can **The dog**

2. ____________________ has a nap.

The snack **The snail**

3. ____________________ is good.

The hats **The pals**

4. ____________________ sit down.

SCHOOL-HOME CONNECTION
Say a naming part of a sentence and have your child complete the sentence.

Name ________________________________

Naming Parts for Two People or Things

The naming part of a sentence can name two people or things.
Sometimes naming parts of two sentences can be joined.

Pig picked apples.

Cat picked apples.

Pig and Cat picked apples.

▶ **Join the naming parts of the sentences. Use the word and. Write the new sentence.**

1. Dog had a nap. Cat had a nap.

____

2. Sam sat down. Pat sat down.

____

SCHOOL-HOME CONNECTION
Say two sentences that end alike. Ask your child to join the naming parts to make a new sentence.

Name ______________________________

Naming Parts for Two People or Things

▶ **Circle the sentence that tells about the picture. Then write the sentence.**

1. Pam had a snack.
   Pam and Mom had a snack.

2. Nick and Hal packed the socks.
   Nick packed the socks.

3. The apples are here.
   The apples and the caps are here.

SCHOOL-HOME CONNECTION
Ask your child to identify the naming part in each sentence.

Name ______________________________

Naming Parts for Two People or Things

▶ **Draw a line to match each sentence to a picture.**

1. Pig had a big surprise.

2. Pig and Duck had a big surprise.

3. Pig and Cat looked at shells.

4. Cat looked at shells.

▶ **Write the correct naming part for the sentence.**

5. ______________________________

are red.

SCHOOL-HOME CONNECTION
Ask your child to read aloud the sentences that name two animals or things.

Name ____________________

Naming Parts for Two People or Things

▶ **Join the naming parts of the sentences. Use the word <u>and</u>. Write the new sentence.**

1. Pam sat. Nick sat.

2. The cat had popcorn. The dog had popcorn.

3. Mack picked apples. Dad picked apples.

4. Dan walked. Kim walked.

SCHOOL-HOME CONNECTION
Ask your child to make up some sentences to show how two naming parts can be joined.

Name ____________________

Telling Parts of Sentences

A sentence has a **telling part.** The telling part tells what someone or something does.

The friends hop.

▶ **Write the telling part of each sentence.**

1. The pig kicks. ____________________

2. The cat naps. ____________________

3. Sam looks. ____________________

4. The clock ticks. ____________________

SCHOOL-HOME CONNECTION
Ask your child to read each sentence and then repeat the sentence with a different telling part.

Name ____________________

Telling Parts of Sentences

▶ **Draw a line between the naming part and the telling part of each sentence. Then write the telling part.**

1. We can sing.

2. The friends skip home.

3. Mom packed a snack.

4. Tim has a hit.

SCHOOL-HOME CONNECTION
Ask your child to complete this sentence with different telling parts: *My friends and I* _____.

Name ______________________________

Telling Parts of Sentences

▶ **Choose a telling part from the boxes for each sentence. Write the telling part in the sentence.**

packed his mitt.	are singing.
had a nap.	can meow.

1. The two pigs ______________________

2. The cat ______________________

3. Nick ______________________

4. The friends ______________________

Harcourt

SCHOOL-HOME CONNECTION
Ask your child to make up a new telling part for each sentence.

Name ____________________

Telling Parts of Sentences

▶ **Write the correct telling part for each sentence.**

sees a map. **can add.**

1. Pam ____________________

sing. **hop.**

2. The friends ____________________

calls home. **walks home.**

3. Ann ____________________

digs. **naps.**

4. The dog ____________________

SCHOOL-HOME CONNECTION
Ask your child to tell why he or she chose the telling part for each sentence.

Name ______________________________

Telling Parts for Two Things

The telling part of a sentence can tell two things that someone or something does.
Sometimes the telling parts of two sentences can be joined.

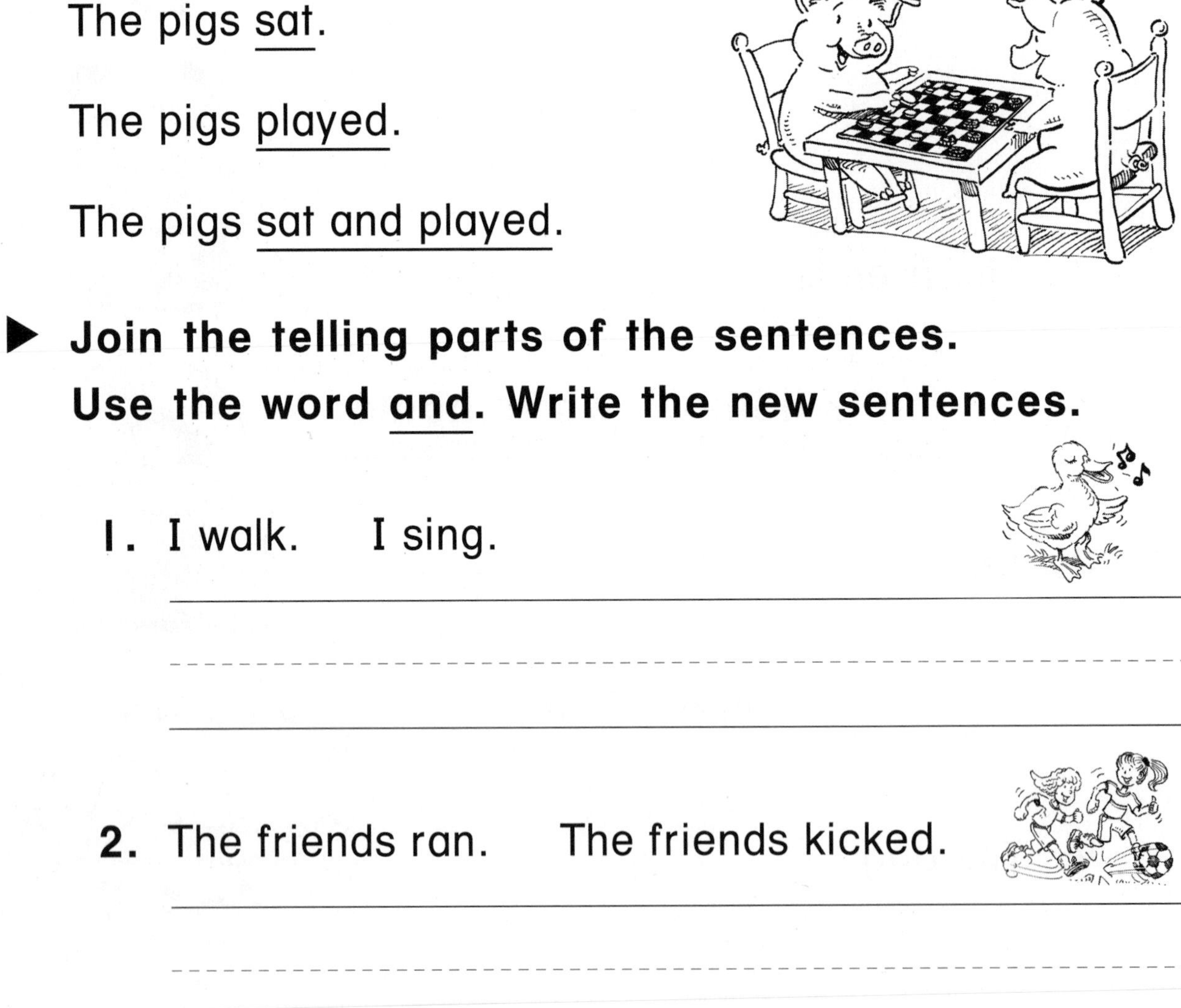

The pigs sat.

The pigs played.

The pigs sat and played.

▶ **Join the telling parts of the sentences. Use the word and. Write the new sentences.**

1. I walk. I sing.

____

2. The friends ran. The friends kicked.

____

SCHOOL-HOME CONNECTION
Say two sentences. Ask your child to join the telling parts to make a new sentence.

Name ___________________________________

Telling Parts for Two Things

▶ **Find two things someone or something is doing in the picture. Circle the sentence that tells about the two things. Then write the sentence.**

1. Two friends shout.
   Two friends play and shout.

   ____

2. The cat hid and looked.
   The cat looked.

   ____

3. Pat sings.
   Pat taps and sings.

   ____

SCHOOL-HOME CONNECTION
Ask your child to tell about two things he or she did at school: *I* ____ *and* ____.

Name ______________________________

Telling Parts for Two Things

▶ **Draw a line to match each sentence to a picture.**

1. Dan stands and packs.

2. The friends sang and walked.

3. Sam ran and kicked.

▶ **Write the correct telling part to complete the sentence.**

sang.	**sat and helped.**	**ran and shouted.**

4. Kim ______________________________

SCHOOL-HOME CONNECTION
Ask your child to make up new telling parts for each sentence.

Name ___

Telling Parts for Two Things

▶ **Join the telling parts of the sentences. Use the word and. Write the new sentences.**

1. Gram sat. Gram napped.

2. Mack ran. Mack shouted.

3. The friends looked. The friends picked.

SCHOOL-HOME CONNECTION
Say two sentences that begin alike. Ask your child to join the telling parts to make a new sentence.

Name ____________________

Complete Sentences

A **sentence** tells a complete thought. It has a naming part and a telling part. It begins with a capital letter. It may end with a **period (.)**, a **question mark (?)**, or an **exclamation point (!)**.

We ran home. I'm home! Are you home?

▶ **Some of these groups of words are sentences. Write the sentences correctly.**

1. a big red apple

____

2. the rabbit has an apple

____

3. is the rabbit happy

____

SCHOOL-HOME CONNECTION
Say some complete and incomplete sentences. Ask your child to identify the complete sentences.

Name ______________________________

Complete Sentences

▶ **Write the sentence from each pair.**

1. I will sing. will sing

2. Did you Did you play tag?

3. Don't kick that can! Don't

4. The dog The dog ran.

SCHOOL-HOME CONNECTION
Ask your child to identify the naming part and the telling part in each complete sentence.

Name ______________________________

Complete Sentences

▶ **Circle the complete sentences. Then write the sentences.**

1. ______________________________

2. ______________________________

3. ______________________________

SCHOOL-HOME CONNECTION
Discuss the end marks. Then have your child read the sentences aloud with expression.

Name ____

Complete Sentences

▶ **Read the naming part and the telling part. Then join the parts to write a complete sentence. Write the sentences correctly.**

1. the cat finds the ball

____

2. the ball is red

____

3. two friends walked home

____

4. we play in the grass

____

SCHOOL-HOME CONNECTION
Ask your child to change the naming part in one sentence and the telling part in another sentence. Have your child say the new sentences.

Name ______________________________

Nouns

Nouns name people, animals, places, or things.

▶ **Write the noun that names people.**

1. My friends walked to the pond. ______________

▶ **Write the noun that names a place.**

2. They like the pond.   ______________

▶ **Write the noun that names an animal.**

3. They saw a fish. ______________

▶ **Write the noun that names a thing.**

4. They tossed a ball. ______________

SCHOOL-HOME CONNECTION
Say some nouns. Ask your child to tell whether each word names a person, animal, place, or thing.

Name ________________________________

Nouns

▶ **Circle the nouns in the sentences. Write two nouns in each list.**

Gram and Bill walk home.

A frog hops into the pond.

The dog sees a stick and a ball.

People

____

____

Animals

____

____

Places

____

____

Things

____

____

SCHOOL-HOME CONNECTION
Ask your child to say some other words for each list.

Name ______________________________

Nouns

▶ **Circle the noun for each picture. Write the word.**

Person

Mom go

____

Place

pond fish

____

Animal

cat nap

____

Thing

apple good

____

SCHOOL-HOME CONNECTION
Ask your child to make up a sentence for each noun.

Name ______________________________

Nouns

▶ **Circle the noun. Write the word in the sentence.**

robin eat

1. I see a ____________.

home big

2. Let's go ____________.

sister soon

3. You are my ____________.

birthday happy

4. It's my ____________.

pond small

5. Can you go to the ____________?

SCHOOL-HOME CONNECTION
Ask your child to complete each sentence with a different noun.

Name ______________________________

Nouns: People or Places

Some **nouns** name people or places.

sister **dad** **pond** **home**

▶ **Write the nouns that name a person and a place in each sentence.**

1. My dad likes to go to the pond.

______________________ ______________________

2. My sister has lots of pets at home.

______________________ ______________________

SCHOOL-HOME CONNECTION
Ask your child to make up a sentence about a person and a place.

Name ______________________________

Nouns: People or Places

▶ **Circle the noun that names each person or place. Write the noun.**

1. man happy

2. pond frog

3. tall sister

4. friend like

5. home big

Harcourt

SCHOOL-HOME CONNECTION
Help your child use both words in a sentence about each person or place.

Name ___________________________________

Nouns: People or Places

▶ **Write a noun for each person or place. Use the words in the boxes.**

pond	sister	mom
forest	home	man

1. ____________

2. ____________

3. ____________

4. ____________

5. ____________

6. ____________

SCHOOL-HOME CONNECTION
Ask your child to name some places he or she would like to visit.

Name ______________________________

Nouns: People or Places

▶ **Trace the girl's path from school. Circle the nouns that name people she sees. Underline the nouns that name places she sees. Write each noun in the correct list.**

People

____

____

____

____

Places

____

____

____

____

SCHOOL-HOME CONNECTION
Talk about the people and places your child saw on the way home from school.

Name ______________________________

Nouns: Animals or Things

Some **nouns** name animals or things.

▶ **Write the noun in each sentence.**

1. My dog is fast. ______________

2. Catch the ball! ______________

3. I eat an apple. ______________

4. The horse is tall. ______________

SCHOOL-HOME CONNECTION
Ask your child to tell whether each noun names an animal or a thing.

Name ______________________________

Nouns: Animals or Things

▶ **Circle the noun that names each animal or thing. Write the noun.**

Harcourt

SCHOOL-HOME CONNECTION
Ask your child to draw a red line under the animals and a blue line under the things.

Name ______________________

Nouns: Animals or Things

▶ **Write a noun that names the animal or thing in the picture. Use the words in the boxes.**

fish	hat	map	dog	banjo

1. Nick has a small ______________.

2. Ellen has two ______________.

3. Ben has a ______________.

4. Kim has a ______________.

5. Dan has a tall ______________.

SCHOOL-HOME CONNECTION
Ask your child to name other animals or things to complete each sentence.

Name ___

Nouns: Animals or Things

▶ **Write a noun for each animal or thing. Use the words in the boxes.**

duck	tent	mat
box	horse	cat

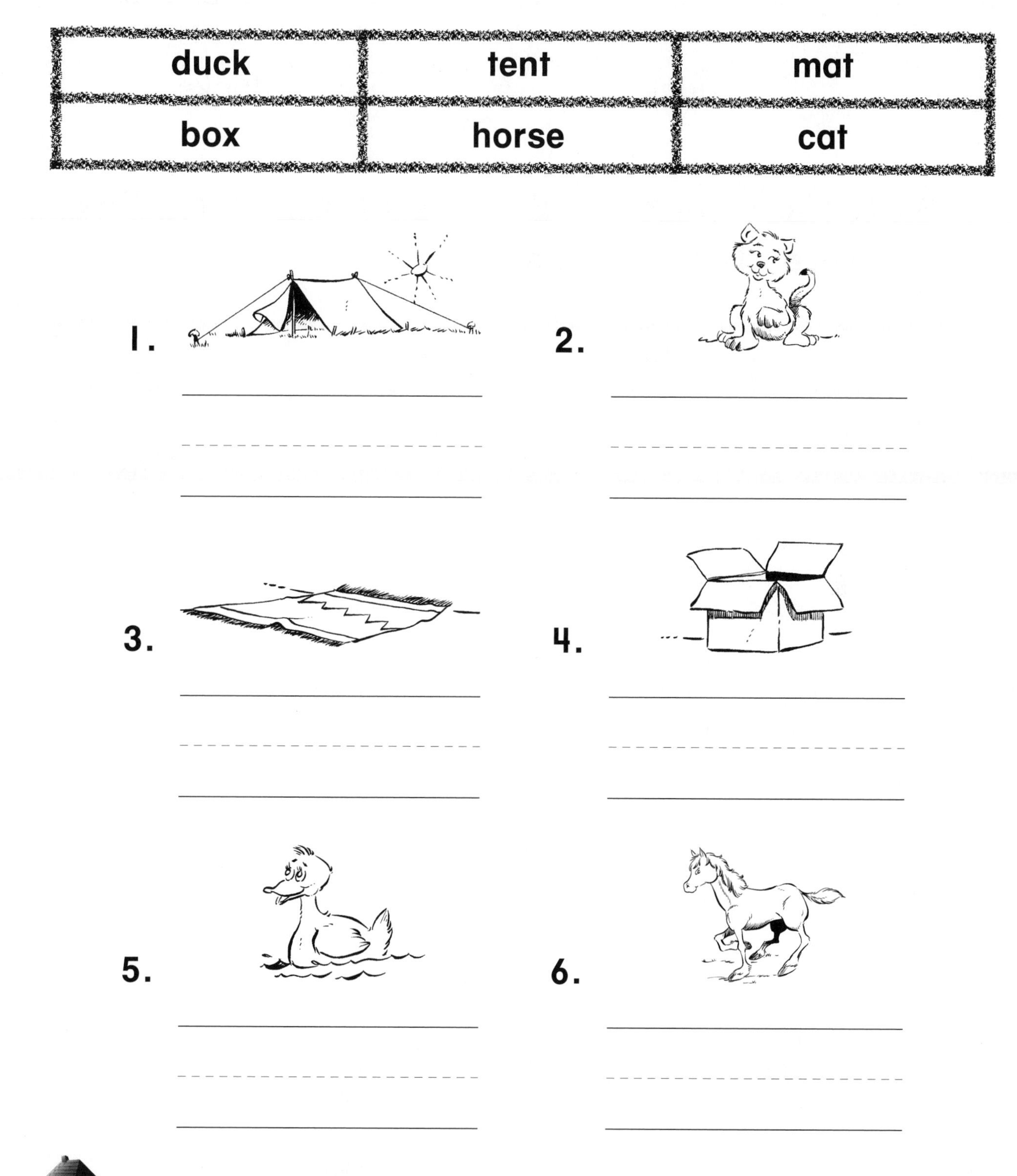

SCHOOL-HOME CONNECTION Help your child make a list of nouns for animals and a list for things.

Name ____________________

One and More Than One

A **noun** can name **one** or **more than one.** Some nouns add s to name more than one.

▶ **Write the noun that tells about the picture. Use the words in the boxes.**

apple	bag	egg	hat
apples	bags	eggs	hats

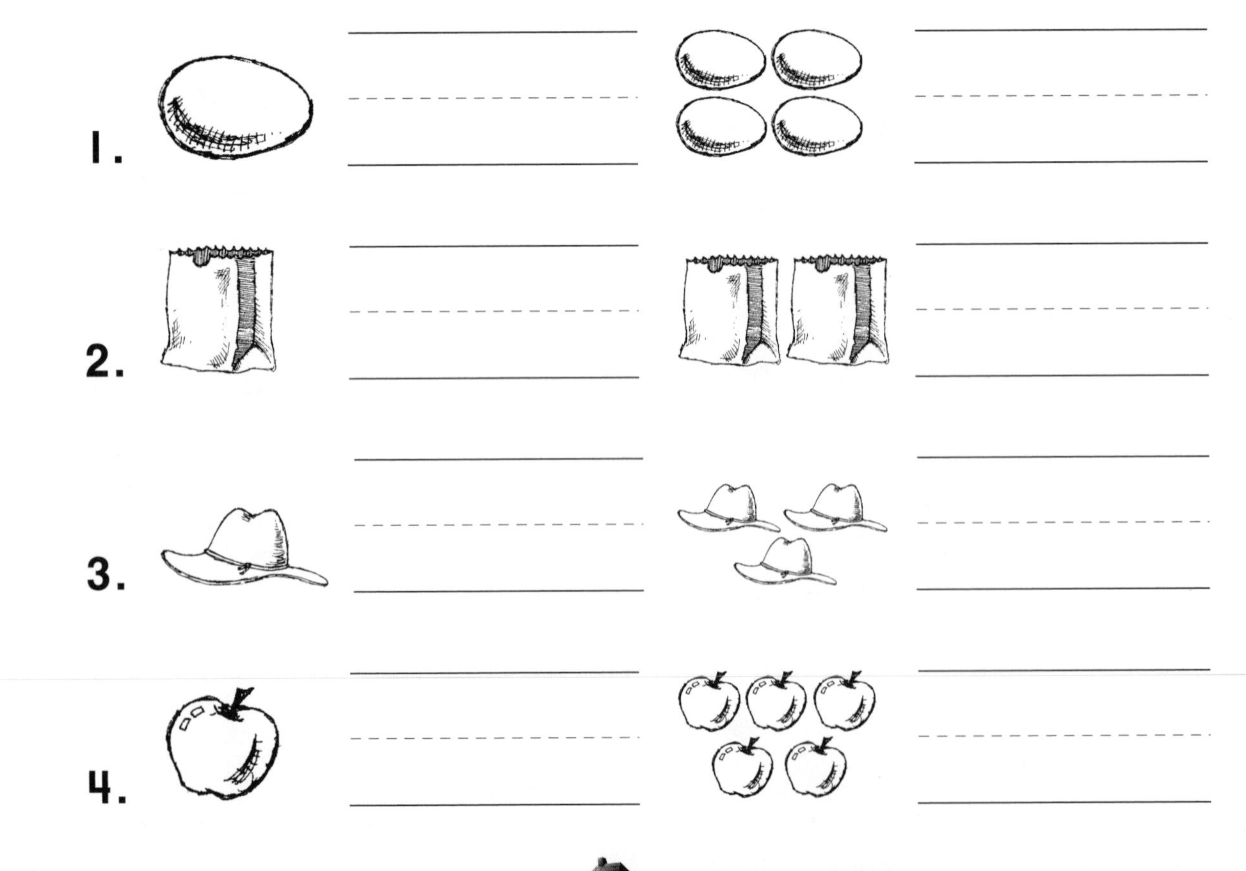

Harcourt

SCHOOL-HOME CONNECTION Write some words that name one thing. Have your child add *s* and read each word.

Name ______________________________

One and More Than One

▶ **Write the noun that tells about the picture.**

rabbit rabbits

1. Here is one ______________________.

pig pigs

2. Here are two ______________________.

frog frogs

3. Here are two ______________________.

bug bugs

4. Here is one ______________________.

cat cats

5. Here are two ______________________.

SCHOOL-HOME CONNECTION
Ask your child to name things at home, such as one table, two chairs, five toys.

Name ___________________________

One and More Than One

▶ **Write the correct noun for each picture. Use the words in the boxes.**

crab	horse	rocks
tree	lamps	hands

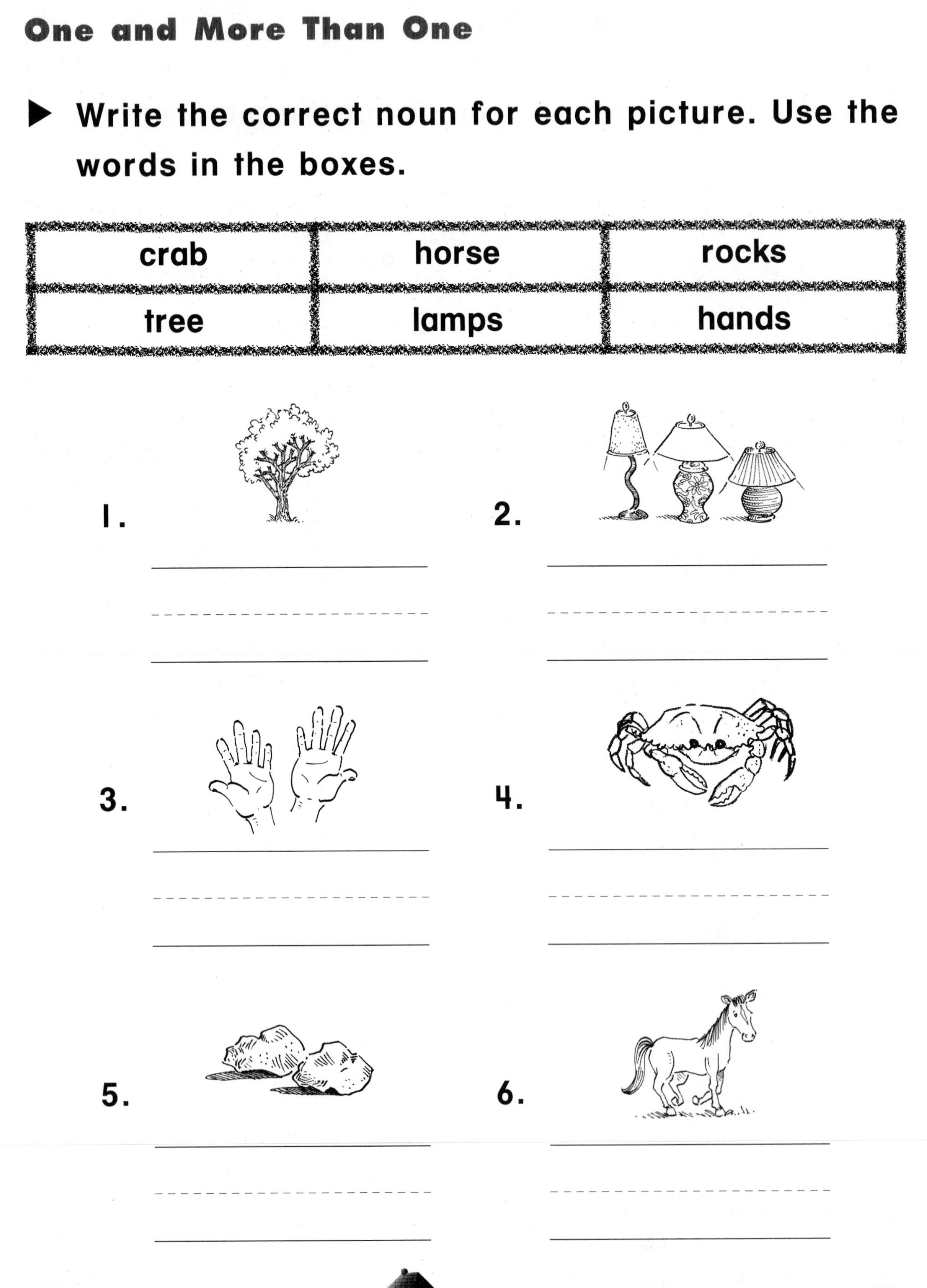

1. ____________

2. ____________

3. ____________

4. ____________

5. ____________

6. ____________

SCHOOL-HOME CONNECTION Say some nouns, such as *book, flower, banana*. Ask your child to say the word that means more than one.

Name ____________________

One and More Than One

▶ **Complete the sentences to tell about the picture. Use the nouns in the boxes.**

ducks	pigs
horse	frogs

1. There is one ____________________.

2. There are two ____________________.

3. There are three ____________________.

4. There are five ____________________.

SCHOOL-HOME CONNECTION
Ask your child to use each noun in another sentence.

Name ______________________________

Special Names and Titles for People

Special names begin with a capital letter. **Special titles** begin with a capital letter.

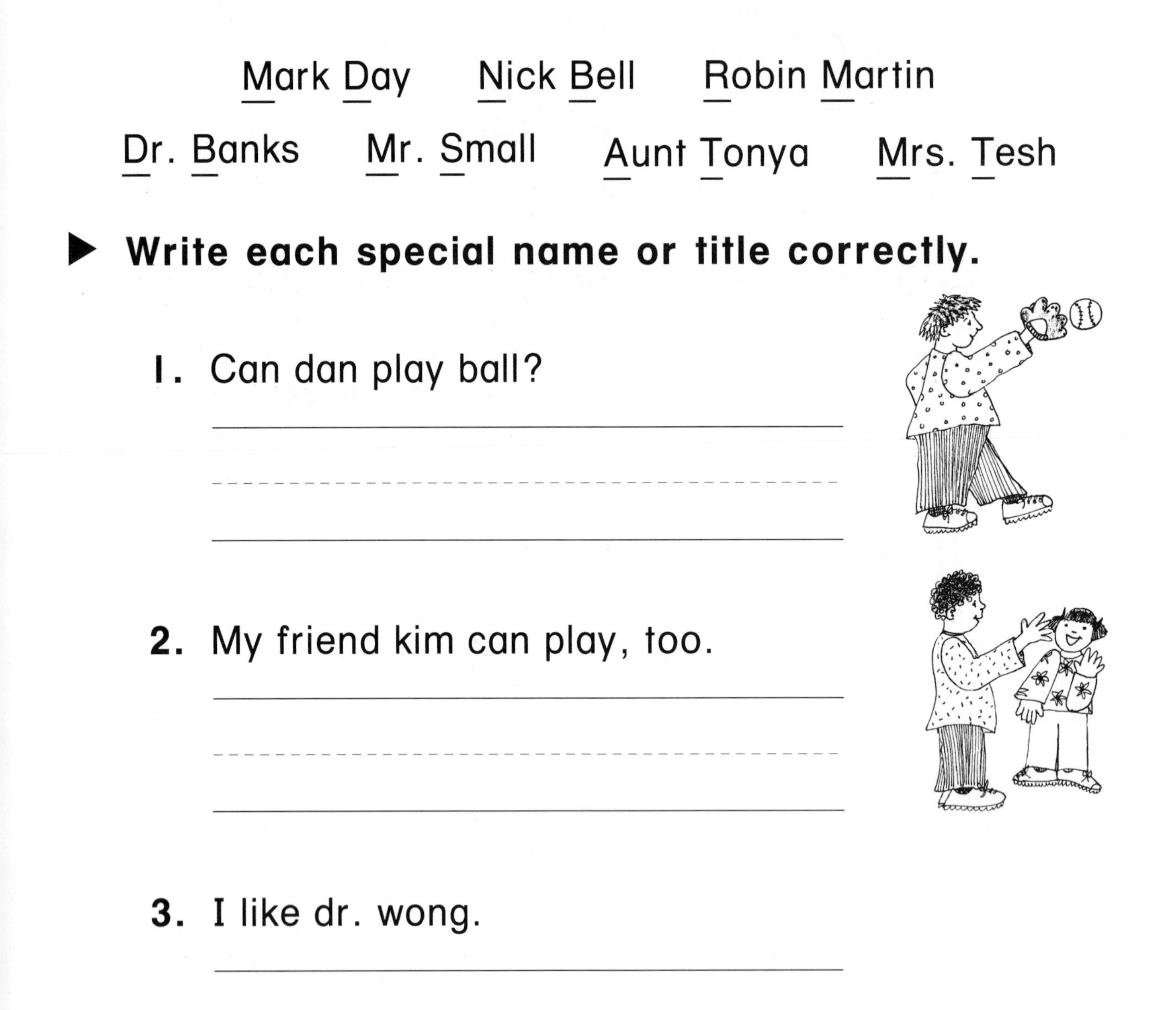

Mark Day   Nick Bell   Robin Martin

Dr. Banks   Mr. Small   Aunt Tonya   Mrs. Tesh

▶ **Write each special name or title correctly.**

1. Can dan play ball?

____

2. My friend kim can play, too.

____

3. I like dr. wong.

____

SCHOOL-HOME CONNECTION Help your child write his or her complete name and your complete name. Add a title, such as *Mr.*, *Mrs.*, *Ms.*, or *Dr.*

Name ______________________________

Special Names and Titles for People

▶ **Circle each special name or title. Match each one to a picture.**

1. Mrs. Block
   woman

2. friend
   Dennis Park

3. Mr. Pintak
   man

▶ **Complete the sentences.**

4. My teacher's name is

   ______________________________.

5. My friend's name is

   ______________________________.

SCHOOL-HOME CONNECTION
Help your child write the first and last names of several friends.

Name ______________________________

Special Names and Titles for People

▶ **Circle the special name or title that is written correctly in each box. Look at the pictures. Write one special name for each sentence.**

tim Tim	uncle alex Uncle Alex	doctor Dr. Marco	Ling ling

1. Can ______________ see my cat now?

2. My friend ______________ likes to fish.

3. My ______________ plays a banjo.

4. How old is ______________?

SCHOOL-HOME CONNECTION
Help your child write the names of family members.

Name ___________________________

Special Names and Titles for People

▶ **Draw a person in each frame. Write a sentence about the person. Use the special name or title for each person.**

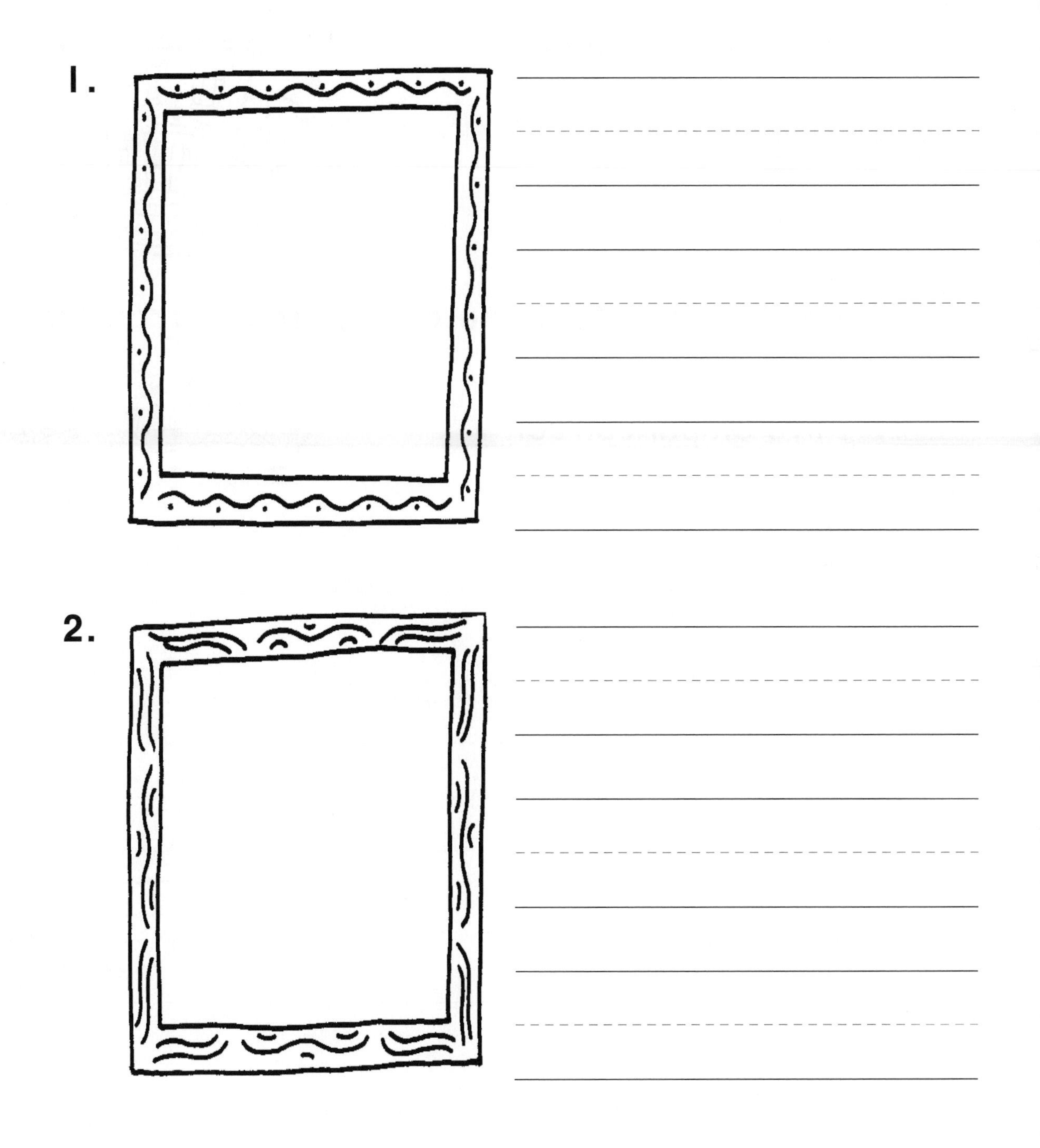

1.

2.

SCHOOL-HOME CONNECTION
Look at family photos with your child. Help her or him write the names of several people.

Name ____________________

Special Names of Places

Special names of places begin with a capital letter.

We go to Mann School.

It is on Bard Street.

It is in Big Fork.

▶ **Write each special name of a place correctly.**

1. I live on park street.

2. My friend lives by grant pond.

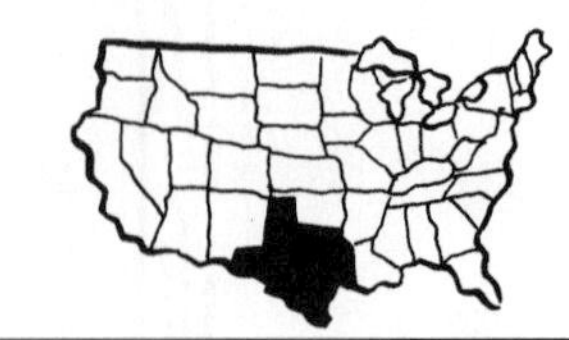

3. We live in texas.

SCHOOL-HOME CONNECTION
Help your child write his or her street address.

Name ___________________________________

Special Names of Places

▶ **Trace the family's path to the beach. Circle the special names of places they see. Write each special name correctly.**

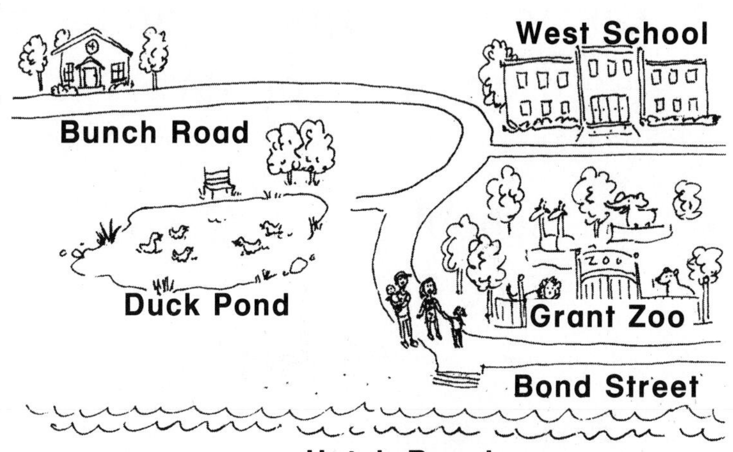

1. bunch road

____

2. west school

____

3. duck pond

____

4. grant zoo

____

5. bond street

____

6. hatch beach

____

SCHOOL-HOME CONNECTION
Help your child write the special names of places he or she likes to visit.

Name ________________________________

Special Names of Places

▶ **Circle each special name of a place. Match each one to a picture.**

1. school
   King School

2. pond
   Clark's Pond

3. road
   Wind Road

4. zoo
   Sand Zoo

▶ **Complete the sentence to tell where you live.**

5. My home is ________________________________

____

________________________________.

SCHOOL-HOME CONNECTION
Help your child write his or her complete address, including the city or town and state.

Name ______________________________

Special Names of Places

▶ Circle each special name of a place. Write each special name below its picture. Then draw something you would see or do in that place.

West Beach	school	Fitch Pond	park
beach	Bond School	pond	Grant Park

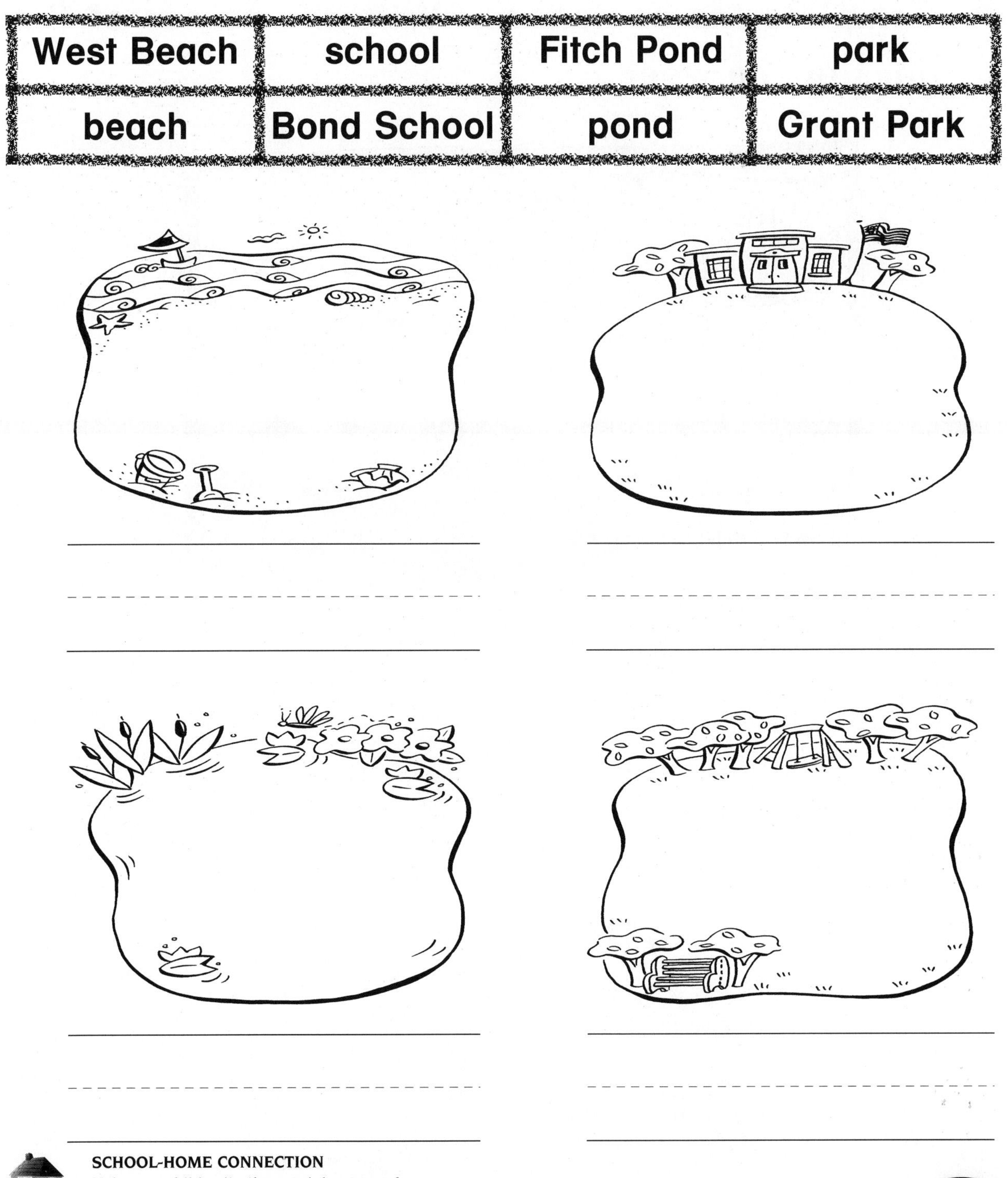

SCHOOL-HOME CONNECTION
Help your child write the special names of places he or she would like to visit someday.

Name ____________________

Names of Days

The names of the **days of the week** begin with capital letters.

▶ **Complete the sentences. Write the names of the days of the week.**

1. Today is ____________________.

2. The next day is ____________________.

3. The day I like best is ____________________.

SCHOOL-HOME CONNECTION
Look at a calendar with your child. Help him or her name the days of the week.

Name ______________________

Names of Days

▶ **Color yellow the spaces that have names of days.**

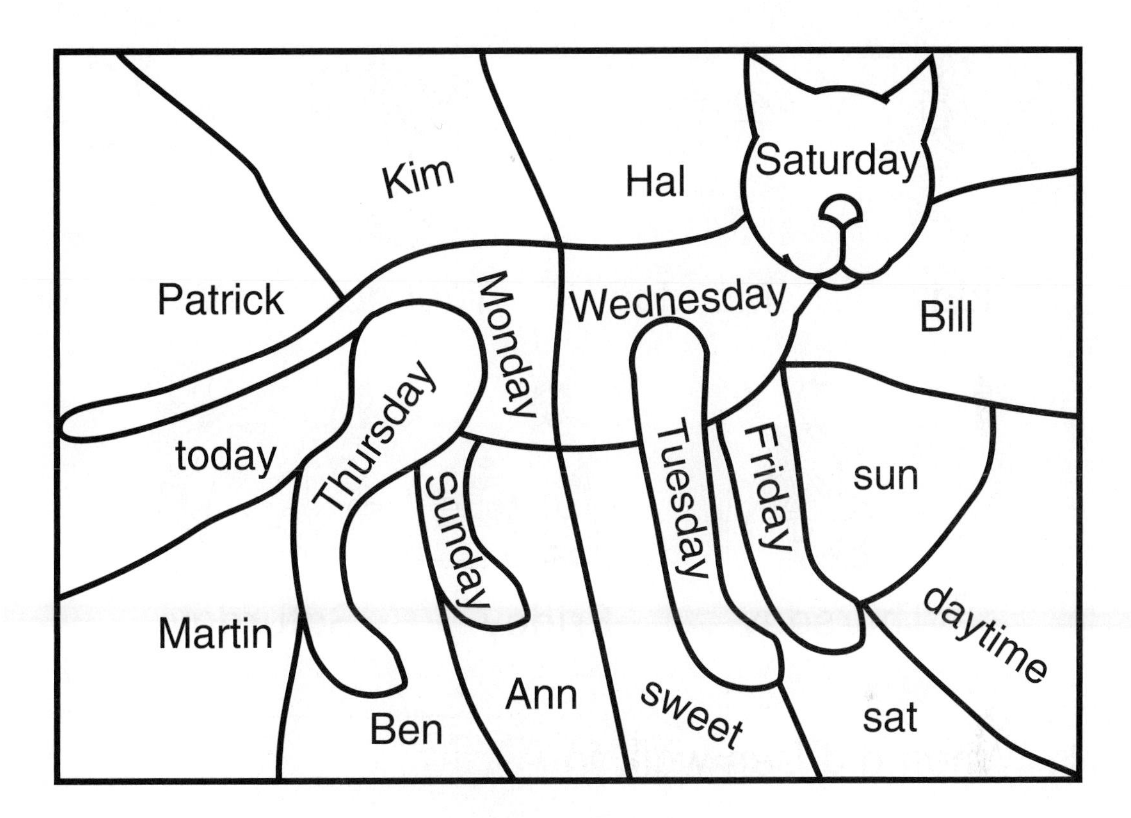

▶ **Complete the sentence.**

1. I see a ______________________.

SCHOOL-HOME CONNECTION
Help your child write the names of the days of the week in order.

Name ______________________________

Names of Days

▶ **Answer each question. Write the correct name of the day.**

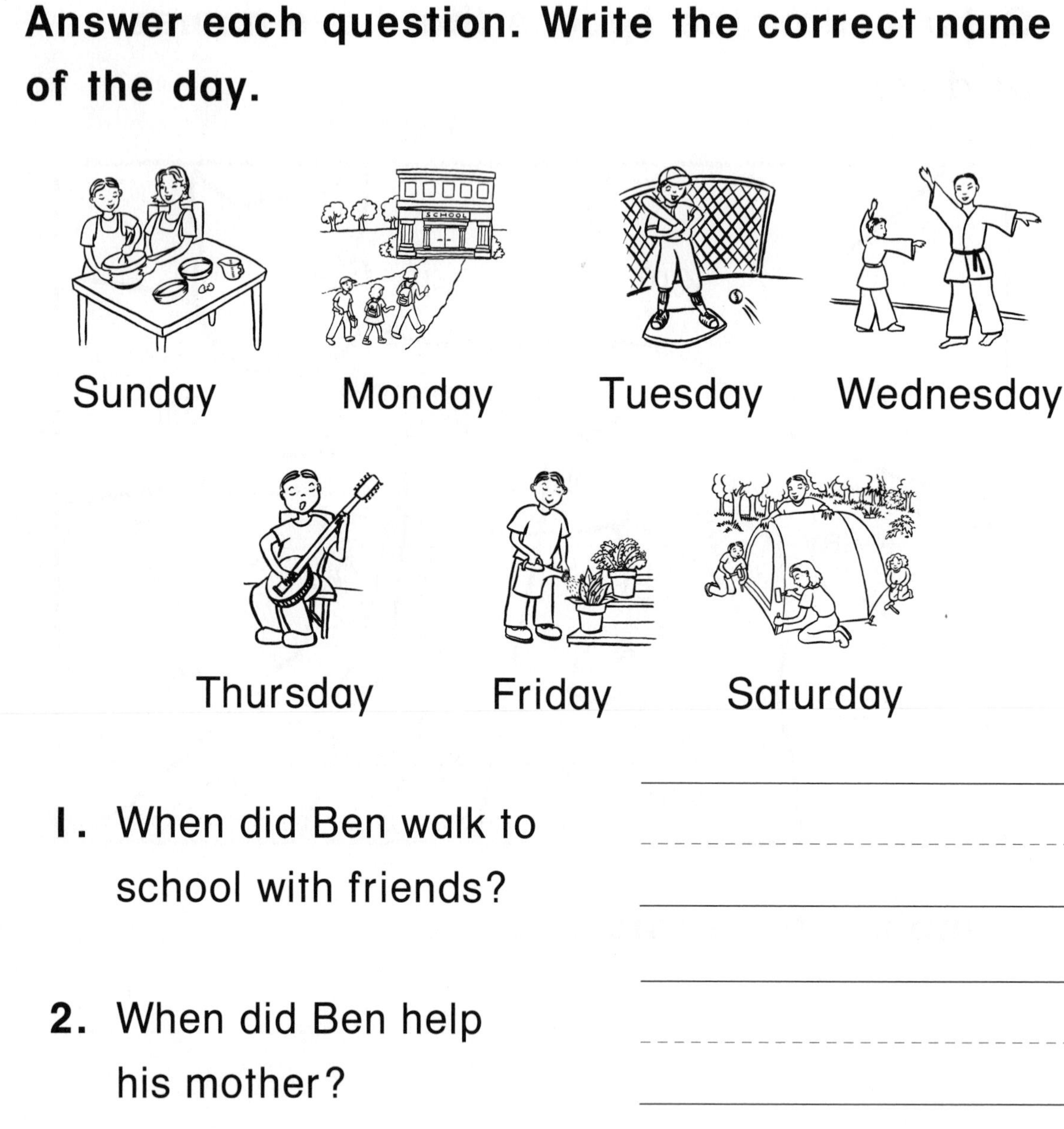

1. When did Ben walk to school with friends? ______________________

2. When did Ben help his mother? ______________________

3. When did Ben play ball? ______________________

4. When did Ben and his family put up a tent? ______________________

SCHOOL-HOME CONNECTION
Ask your child to tell what Ben did on the other days of the week.

Name ______________________

Names of Days

▶ **Write the name of a day to complete each sentence.**

My Week

Sunday	Monday	Tuesday	Wednesday	Thursday	Friday	Saturday
1 play ball	2 go to Nick's house	3 watch TV	4 see Gram	5 find rocks	6 call Kim	7 ★ get a pet

1. I watch TV on ______________________.

2. I see Gram on ______________________.

3. I call Kim on ______________________.

4. I get a pet on ______________________.

5. I play ball on ______________________.

SCHOOL-HOME CONNECTION
Ask your child to write the days of the week.
Discuss what he or she might do on each day.

Name ____________________

Names of Months

The names of the **months** begin with capital letters.

▶ **Write the name of a month to complete each sentence.**

1. This month is ____________________.

2. My birthday is in ____________________.

SCHOOL-HOME CONNECTION
Help your child write the complete date of her or his birthday.

Name ______________________________

Names of Months

▶ **Write the name of a month to complete each sentence.**

1. The first month is ______________________.

2. The last month is ______________________.

3. I like ______________________ the best.

SCHOOL-HOME CONNECTION
Discuss why the month named is your child's favorite month.

Name ______________________________

Names of Months

▶ **Write the name of each month correctly.**

1. may
2. november
3. july
4. january
5. february
6. august

Harcourt

SCHOOL-HOME CONNECTION
Have your child name the months of the year in order.

Name ____________________

Names of Months

▶ **Complete each sentence with the name of a month.**

1. My birthday is in ____________________.

2. My friend's birthday is in ____________________.

3. My teacher's birthday is in ____________________.

SCHOOL-HOME CONNECTION
Help your child write the birthdates of other family members.

Name ______________________________

Names of Holidays

The names of **holidays** begin with capital letters.

Today is February 14.

It is Valentine's Day.

▶ **Write the name of each holiday correctly.**

1. I get cards on valentine's day.

____

2. My brother plays in a band on memorial day.

____

3. We eat at Gram's house on thanksgiving day.

____

SCHOOL-HOME CONNECTION
Discuss your child's favorite holiday and why it is his or her favorite.

Name ______________________________

Names of Holidays

▶ **Circle the correct way to write the name of each holiday. Then write it.**

1. new year's day
   New Year's Day

____

2. Thanksgiving Day
   thanksgiving day

____

3. independence day
   Independence Day

____

SCHOOL-HOME CONNECTION
Help your child write the name of his or her favorite holiday.

Name ______________________________

Names of Holidays

▶ **Match each picture with the name of the holiday. Then complete the sentence.**

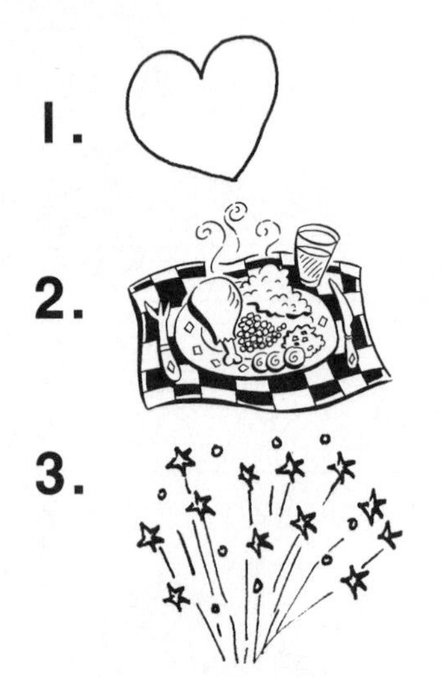

1\. 2. 3.

Independence Day

Thanksgiving Day

Valentine's Day

The holiday I like best is

______________________________.

▶ **Draw a picture that shows what you like to do on this holiday.**

SCHOOL-HOME CONNECTION
Discuss your child's picture. Ask why she or he likes the activity.

Name ______________________________

Names of Holidays

▶ **Write the name of each holiday correctly.**

1. We visit Gram on thanksgiving day.

2. We send cards on valentine's day.

3. We see a band on memorial day.

4. We put out our flag on flag day.

SCHOOL-HOME CONNECTION
Flip through a calendar with your child. Point out the holidays that occur in the various months.

Name ______________________

Using I and Me

The words **I** and **me** take the place of your own name. Use **I** in the naming part of a sentence. Use **me** in the telling part of a sentence. The word **I** is always written as a capital letter.

I had a birthday.

My friends surprised me.

▶ **Write I or me to complete each sentence.**

1. ______________ am seven today.

2. This box is for ______________.

3. My Gram gave ______________ a pup.

4. ______________ call my pup Fred.

Harcourt

SCHOOL-HOME CONNECTION
Ask your child to use the words *I* and *me* in sentences.

Name ___________________________________

Using I and Me

▶ **Circle the correct word. Then write it in the sentence.**

I me

1. ______________ like to write.

I me

2. My big brother helps ______________.

I me

3. He reads to ______________ at night.

I me

4. ______________ write about animals.

I me

5. ______________ like horses the best.

SCHOOL-HOME CONNECTION
Help your child write sentences using the words *I* and *me*.

Name ______________________________

Using I and Me

▶ **Circle I or me to complete each sentence. Then write the sentence correctly.**

1. ___ like pets. **I** **me**

2. Fish are the best pets for ___. **I** **me**

3. ___ keep ten fish in my room. **I** **me**

4. Dad helps ___ feed the fish. **I** **me**

SCHOOL-HOME CONNECTION
Ask your child to use the words *I* and *me* to tell about a pet.

Name ____________________

Using I and Me

▶ **Write I or me. Circle a picture.**

What Am I?

1. ______ float in the sea.

2. ______ can't move on land.

3. You can ride on ______.

SCHOOL-HOME CONNECTION
Help your child write a riddle using the words *I* and *me*.

Name ___________________________

Using He, She, It, and They

The words **he**, **she**, **it**, and **they** take the place of some nouns.

Use **he** for a man or a boy.
Use **she** for a woman or a girl.
Use **it** for an animal or a thing.
Use **they** for more than one person, animal, or thing.

He made a snack. They will eat it.

▶ **Write he, she, it, or they to complete each sentence.**

1. ______________ like to bake cakes.

2. Today ______________ baked a fruit cake.

3. ______________ liked ______________!

Harcourt

SCHOOL-HOME CONNECTION
Ask your child to use *he*, *she*, *it*, and *they* in sentences.

Name ______________________________

Using He, She, It, and They

▶ **Write he, she, it, or they to take the place of the noun or nouns in each sentence.**

1. Pam sits in the tent.

   ____________ sits in the tent.

2. The tent has two sides.

   ____________ has two sides.

3. The children are friends.

   ____________ are friends.

4. Tess and Marco think the tent is fun!

   ____________ think the tent is fun!

5. Marco is grinning.

   ____________ is grinning.

SCHOOL-HOME CONNECTION
As you read the page with your child, ask him or her to circle the word or words that *he, she, it,* and *they* refer to.

Name ______________________________

Using He, She, It, and They

▶ **What word can take the place of the nouns in each list? Write he, she, it, or they under each cake.**

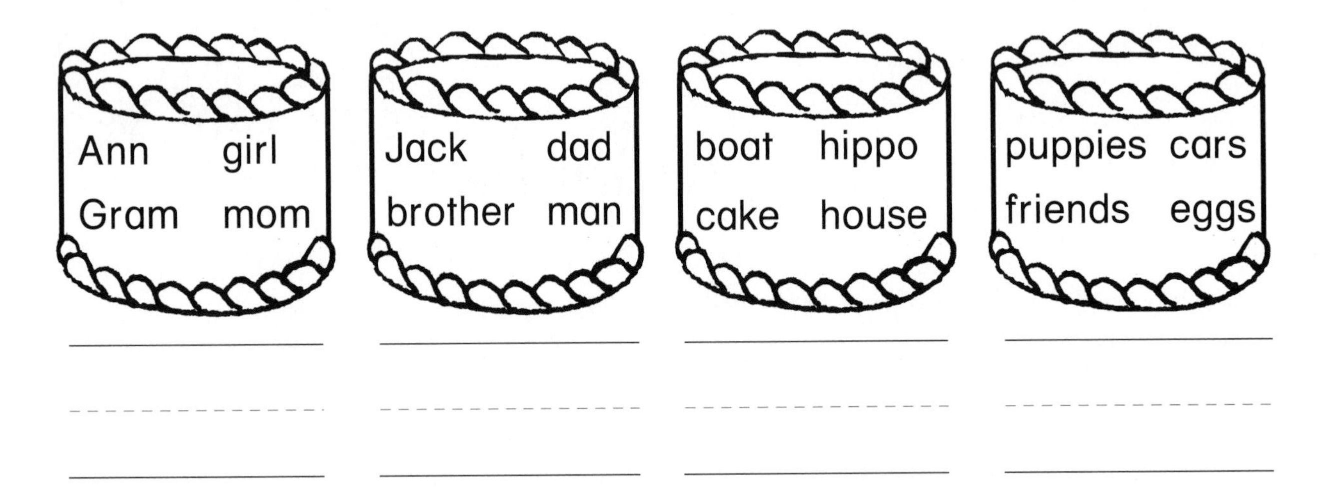

________________ ________________ ________________ ________________

▶ **Write this sentence using he, she, it, or they.**

The birthday cake is very sweet!

____

SCHOOL-HOME CONNECTION
Say a sentence with one of the words in each cake. Ask your child to repeat the sentence using *he*, *she*, *it*, or *they*.

Name ______________________________

Using He, She, It, and They

▶ **Write he, she, it, or they to take the place of the underlined word or words in each sentence.**

1. Jenny lost her hippo. ____________

2. Dad helped Jenny look. ____________

3. Dad and Jenny looked all day. ____________

4. Dad found the hippo in a tree. ____________

5. Jenny was so happy! ____________

SCHOOL-HOME CONNECTION
Ask your child to explain why she or he wrote *he, she, it,* or *they* for each sentence.

Name ______________________________

Describing Words: Feelings

A **describing word** tells about a naming word. Some describing words tell how people **feel**.

Katie catches a little fish.
Now she is glad.

▶ **Circle the describing words. Then write each one.**

1. long legs
2. wet dog
3. happy baby
4. sweet snack

SCHOOL-HOME CONNECTION
Ask your child to use describing words to tell about items in your home.

Name ______________________________

Describing Words: Feelings

▶ **Write the describing word in each sentence.**

1. This cat has a long tail.

2. This rabbit has pink eyes.

3. This dog gives a wet kiss.

4. This fish has big eyes.

5. This is a happy family.

SCHOOL-HOME CONNECTION Ask your child to think of another describing word for each sentence.

Name ______________________________

Describing Words: Feelings

▶ **Write the describing words that tell how Jane feels.**

1. When Jane is happy, she giggles.

____

2. When Jane is tired, she sleeps.

____

3. When Jane is hungry, she eats.

____

4. When Jane is sad, she hugs her mom.

____

5. When Jane is hot, she finds a fan.

____

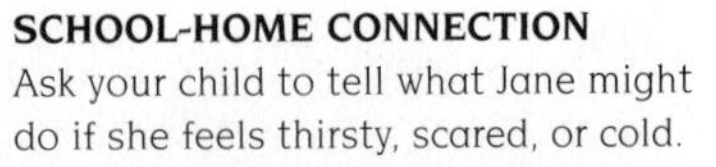

SCHOOL-HOME CONNECTION
Ask your child to tell what Jane might do if she feels thirsty, scared, or cold.

Name ______________________________

Describing Words: Feelings

▶ **Use the describing words in the boxes to tell about the picture.**

wet	fat	sad
tall	hot	

1. ______________________ trees

2. ______________________ sun

3. ______________________ children

4. ______________________ dog

5. ______________________ baby

SCHOOL-HOME CONNECTION
Ask your child to use describing words to tell about her or his favorite toys.

Name ______________________________

Describing Words: Color, Size, Shape

Some describing words tell about **color.**
Some describing words tell about **size** or **shape.**

Color
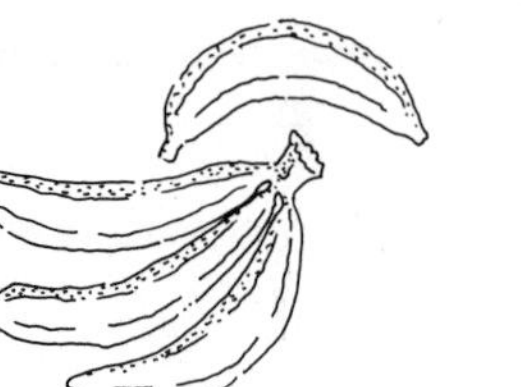
yellow

Size
big

Shape

round

▶ **Answer each question. Write the describing word that tells about color, size, or shape.**

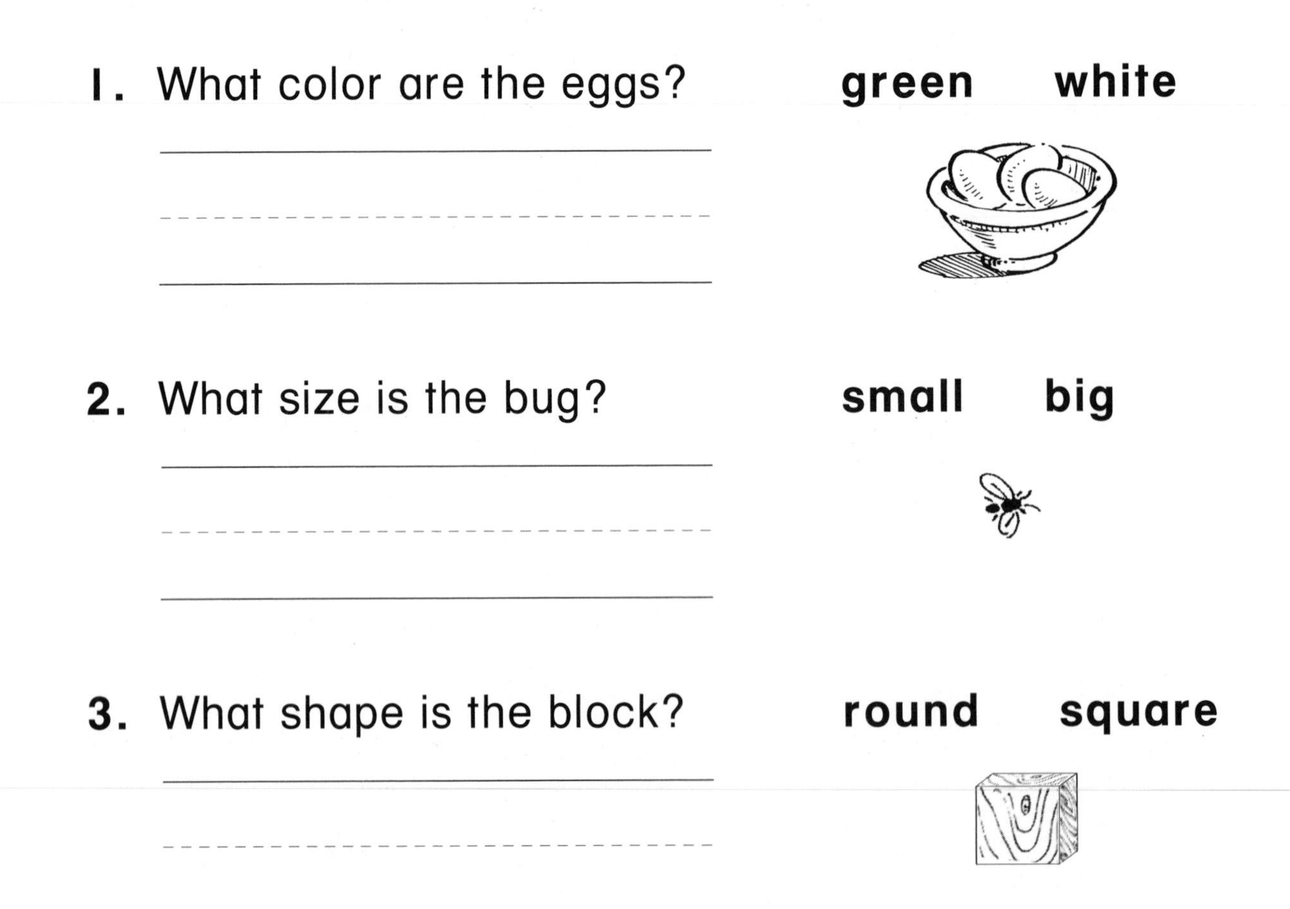

1. What color are the eggs? **green** **white**

____

2. What size is the bug? **small** **big**

____

3. What shape is the block? **round** **square**

____

SCHOOL-HOME CONNECTION Ask your child to describe the color, size, and shape of various objects at home.

Name ______________________________

Describing Words: Color, Size, Shape

▶ Write a different color word from the boxes under each ball. Then color the balls to match the words.

red	yellow	blue
green	orange	brown

▶ Circle the words that describe size and shape. Then finish the sentence with a describing word that tells your favorite color.

I like balls that are big, round, and ______________.

SCHOOL-HOME CONNECTION
Ask your child to use describing words to tell the size, shape, and color of one object in the room.

Name ______________________________

Describing Words: Color, Size, Shape

▶ **Use the picture and the words in the boxes to complete each sentence.**

square	round
small	big

1. The box is ______________________.

2. The ball is ______________________.

3. The cat is ______________________.

4. The dog is ______________________.

SCHOOL-HOME CONNECTION
Ask your child to tell whether each word describes a color, a shape, or a size.

Name ____________________

Describing Words: Color, Size, Shape

▶ **Write a describing word for each picture.**

round	little	square
big	green	brown

1. ____________________

2. ____________________

3. ____________________

4. ____________________

5. ____________________

6. ____________________

SCHOOL-HOME CONNECTION
Ask your child to think of another describing word for each picture.

Name ______________________________

Describing Words: Taste, Smell, Sound, Feel

Some describing words tell how things **taste** or **smell.**
Some describing words tell how things **sound.**
Some describing words tell how things **feel.**

Lemons taste sour. They feel hard.
They smell fresh.

▶ **Write the word that describes how something tastes, smells, sounds, or feels.**

1. The cake tastes sweet.

2. The fruit smells fresh.

3. The horn is so loud!

4. The puppy feels soft.

SCHOOL-HOME CONNECTION
Ask your child to use the describing words to tell about some other things.

Name ______________________________

Describing Words: Taste, Smell, Sound, Feel

▶ **Write a describing word from the boxes for each sentence.**

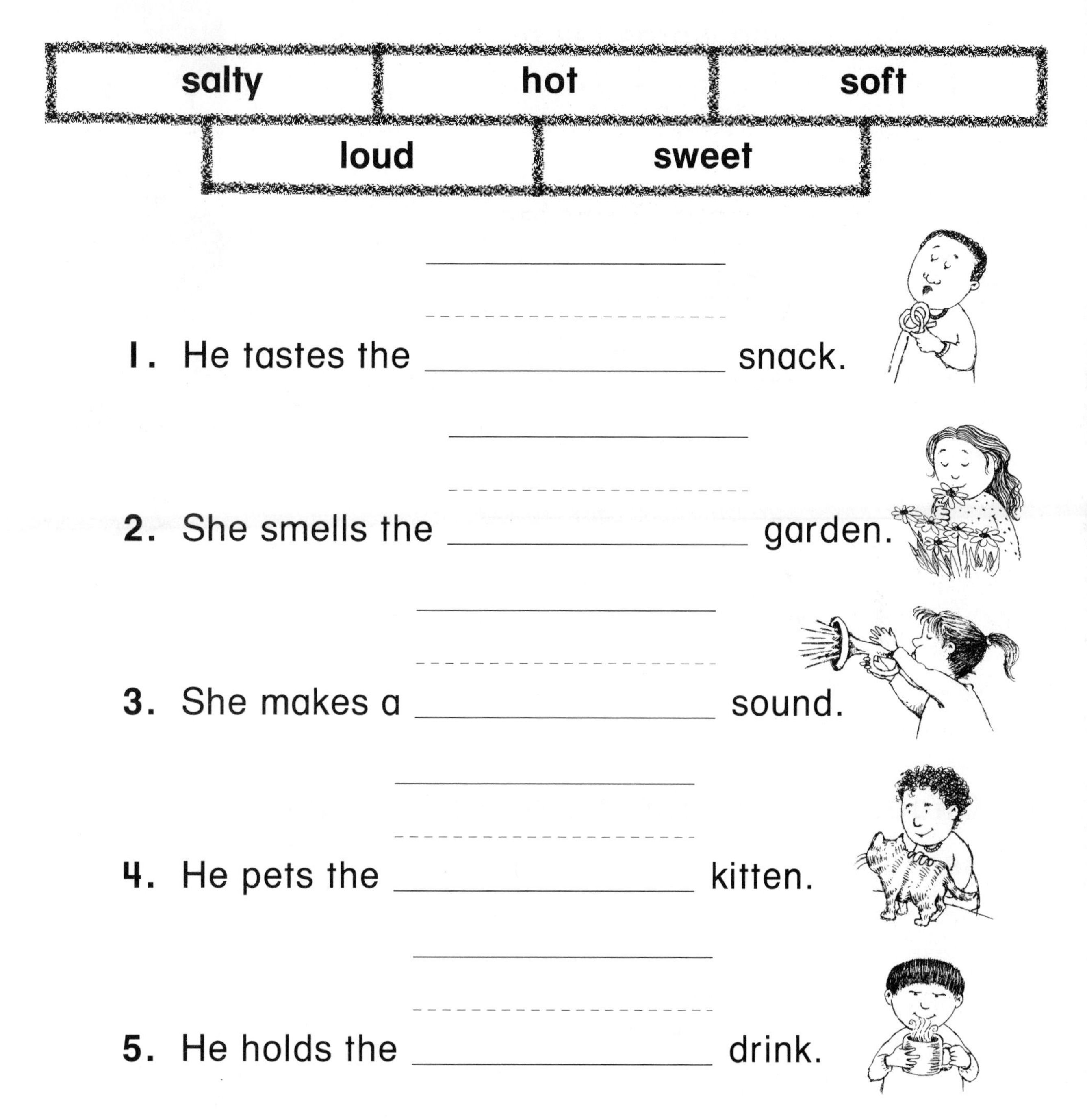

salty	hot	soft
loud	sweet	

1. He tastes the ______________ snack.

2. She smells the ______________ garden.

3. She makes a ______________ sound.

4. He pets the ______________ kitten.

5. He holds the ______________ drink.

SCHOOL-HOME CONNECTION
Ask your child to tell how various objects at home taste, smell, sound, or feel.

Name ______________________________

Describing Words: Taste, Smell, Sound, Feel

▶ **Draw a line to match the words in each box with the correct title.**

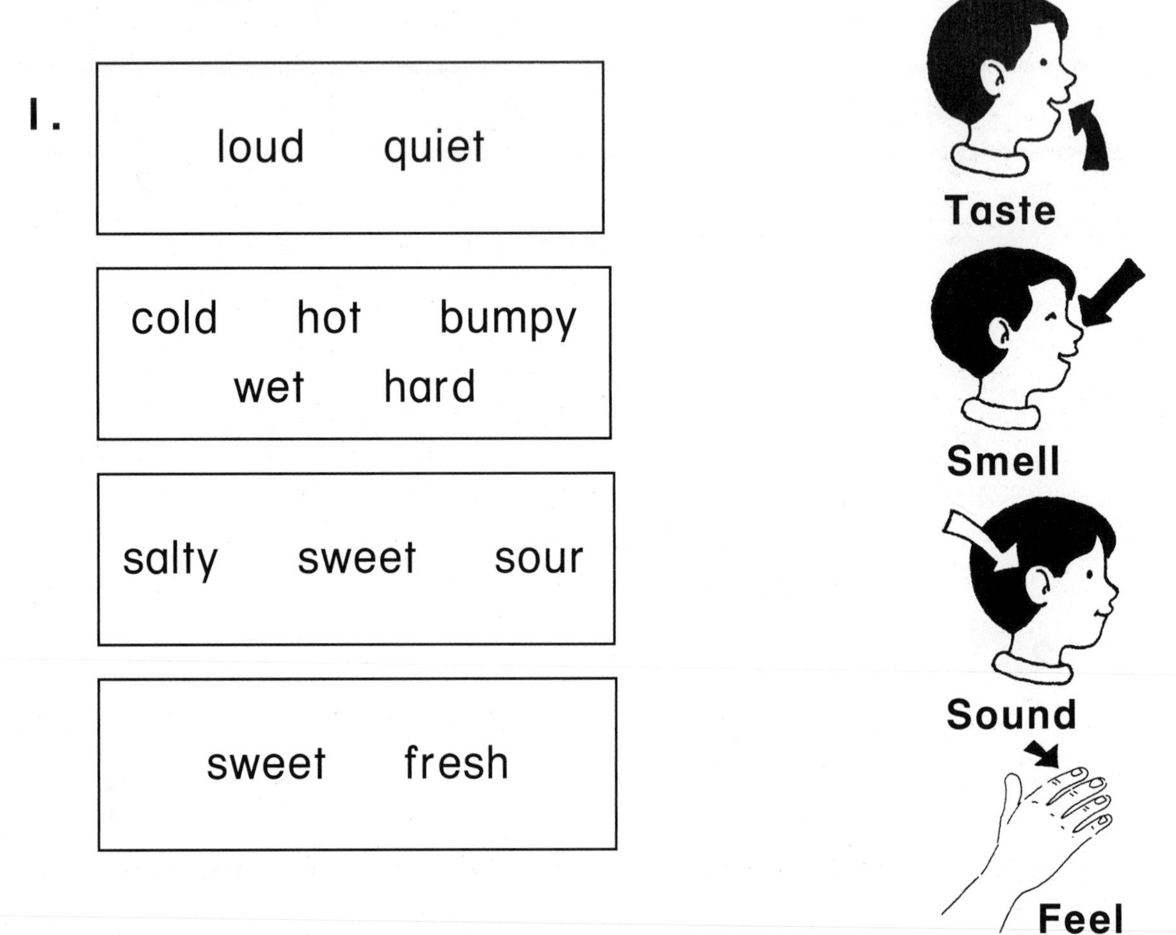

▶ **Choose two of the words to complete this sentence.**

2. Ice cream is ______________ and ______________.

Harcourt

SCHOOL-HOME CONNECTION
Ask your child to describe how popcorn tastes, smells, sounds, and feels.

Name ___________________________

Describing Words: Taste, Smell, Sound, Feel

▶ **Use words from the boxes to complete each sentence.**

wet	sticky	quiet
sweet	fresh	sour

1. The park smells ________________.

The park sounds ________________.

2. The cake tastes ________________.

The cake feels ________________.

3. The drink feels ________________.

The drink tastes ________________.

SCHOOL-HOME CONNECTION
Name a variety of things. Ask your child to tell how they taste, smell, sound, or feel.

Name ______________________________

Describing Words: How Many

Some describing words tell **how many**.

one

two

three

▶ **Complete each sentence with a number. Use the pictures to help you.**

1. Jenny bakes ______________ cakes.

2. Mike pets ______________ rabbits.

3. Jack reads ______________ book.

4. Mom cooks ______________ onions.

SCHOOL-HOME CONNECTION
Ask your child to use numbers to describe things at home; for example, five chairs, one TV, three windows.

Name ________________________________

Describing Words: How Many

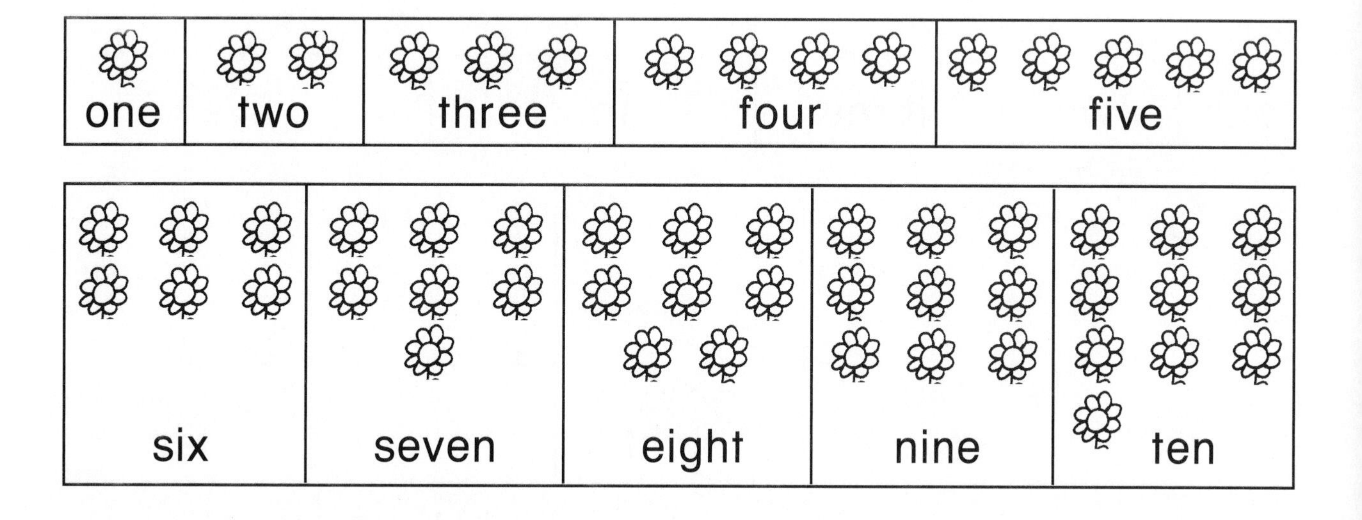

▶ **Write a number word to tell how many.**

1. ________________________

2. ________________________

3. ________________________

4. ________________________

5. ________________________

6. ________________________

SCHOOL-HOME CONNECTION
Ask your child to draw pictures for the number words he or she did not write.

Name ______________________________

Describing Words: How Many

one	two	three	four	five

six	seven	eight	nine	ten

▶ **Answer each question about the picture. Write the number word.**

1. How many hippos? ______________

2. How many snakes? ______________

3. How many kangaroos? ______________

4. How many tigers? ______________

SCHOOL-HOME CONNECTION
Ask your child to write the number word that tells how many bears are in the picture.

Name ____________________

Describing Words: How Many

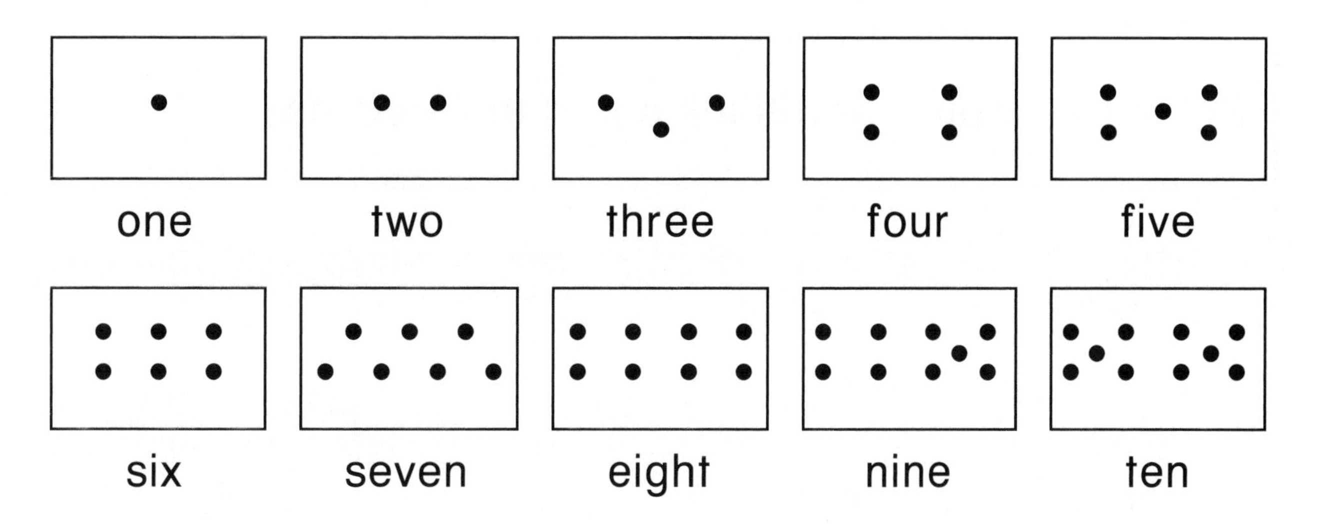

▶ **Draw a line to match each number word to the correct picture.**

1. one

2. eight

3. five

4. four

5. three

6. seven

SCHOOL-HOME CONNECTION
Ask your child to write the following sentence and complete it with a number word: *I am __ years old.*

Name ____________________

Describing Words: Weather

Some describing words tell about the **weather**.

sunny	rainy	snowy	cloudy

▶ **Complete each sentence with a describing word about the weather.**

1. We go to the beach on a ____________ day.

2. We like to skate on a ____________ day.

3. We get wet on a ____________ day.

4. We read books on a ____________ day.

SCHOOL-HOME CONNECTION
Ask your child to use describing words to tell about the current weather.

Name ____________________

Describing Words: Weather

▶ **Circle each correct weather word. Then write the word in the sentence.**

1. It is so hot! **sunny cloudy**

   It is a ____________ day.

2. It is so wet! **sunny rainy**

   It is a ____________ day.

3. It is so dark! **cloudy sunny**

   It is a ____________ day.

4. It is so cold! **rainy snowy**

   It is a ____________ day.

SCHOOL-HOME CONNECTION
Ask your child to use a similar sentence pattern to tell about today's weather.

Name ______________________________

Describing Words: Weather

▶ **Write a word from the boxes that describes the weather in each picture.**

windy	snowy
rainy	sunny

SCHOOL-HOME CONNECTION
Ask your child to choose a picture and tell what she or he likes to do on such a day.

Name ______________________________

Describing Words: Weather

▶ **Underline the weather word in each sentence. Then draw a line to match the sentence with a picture.**

1. On snowy days we go sledding.

2. On rainy days we splash.

3. On windy days we fly our kites.

4. What kind of weather do you like best?

____

____

▶ **Draw a picture of today's weather.**

SCHOOL-HOME CONNECTION
Discuss item 4 with your child. Ask why he or she likes that kind of weather.

Name ______________________________

Describing Words: -er and -est

Some describing words tell how one thing is different from one other thing. Add -er to tell how it is different.

Some describing words tell how one thing is different from two or more other things. Add -est to tell how it is different.

 tall 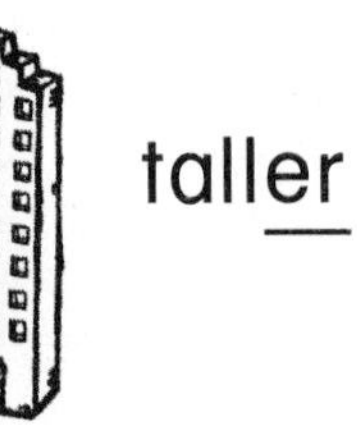 taller  tallest

▶ **Write long, longer, or longest to complete each sentence.**

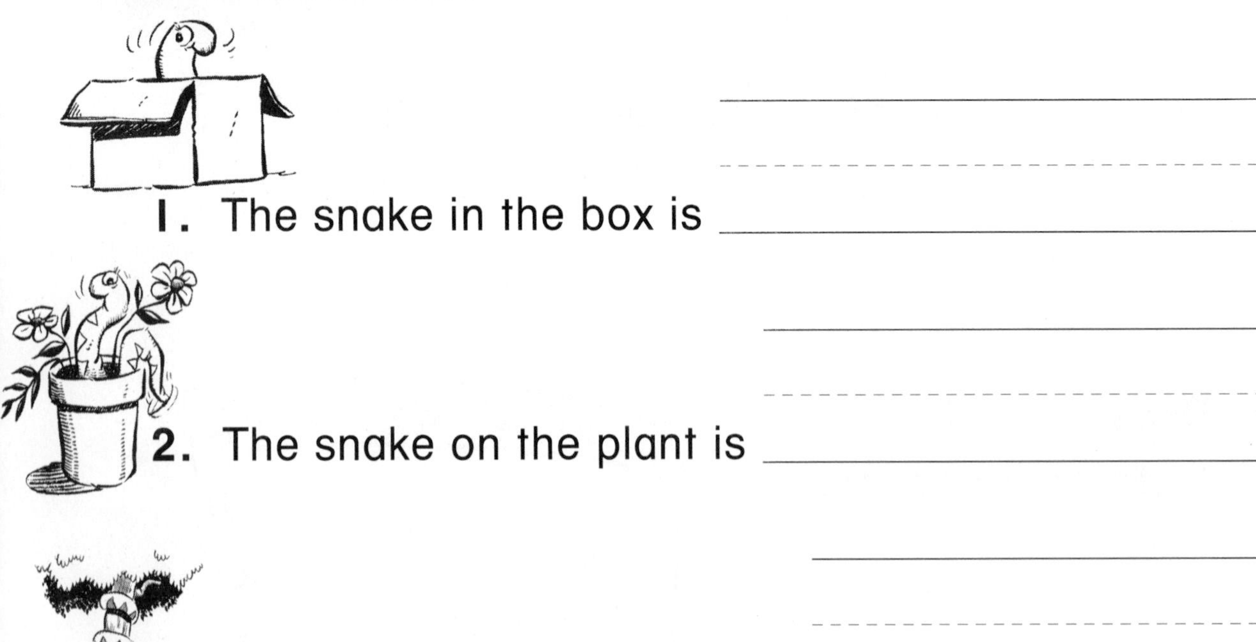

1. The snake in the box is ______________.

2. The snake on the plant is ______________.

3. The snake in the tree is the ______________ of all.

SCHOOL-HOME CONNECTION
Ask your child to use the words *tall*, *taller*, and *tallest* in sentences.

Name ___________________________

Describing Words: -er and -est

▶ **Draw three pictures to show how three animals compare in size. Use the words from one box to label your pictures.**

small	smaller	smallest

big	bigger	biggest

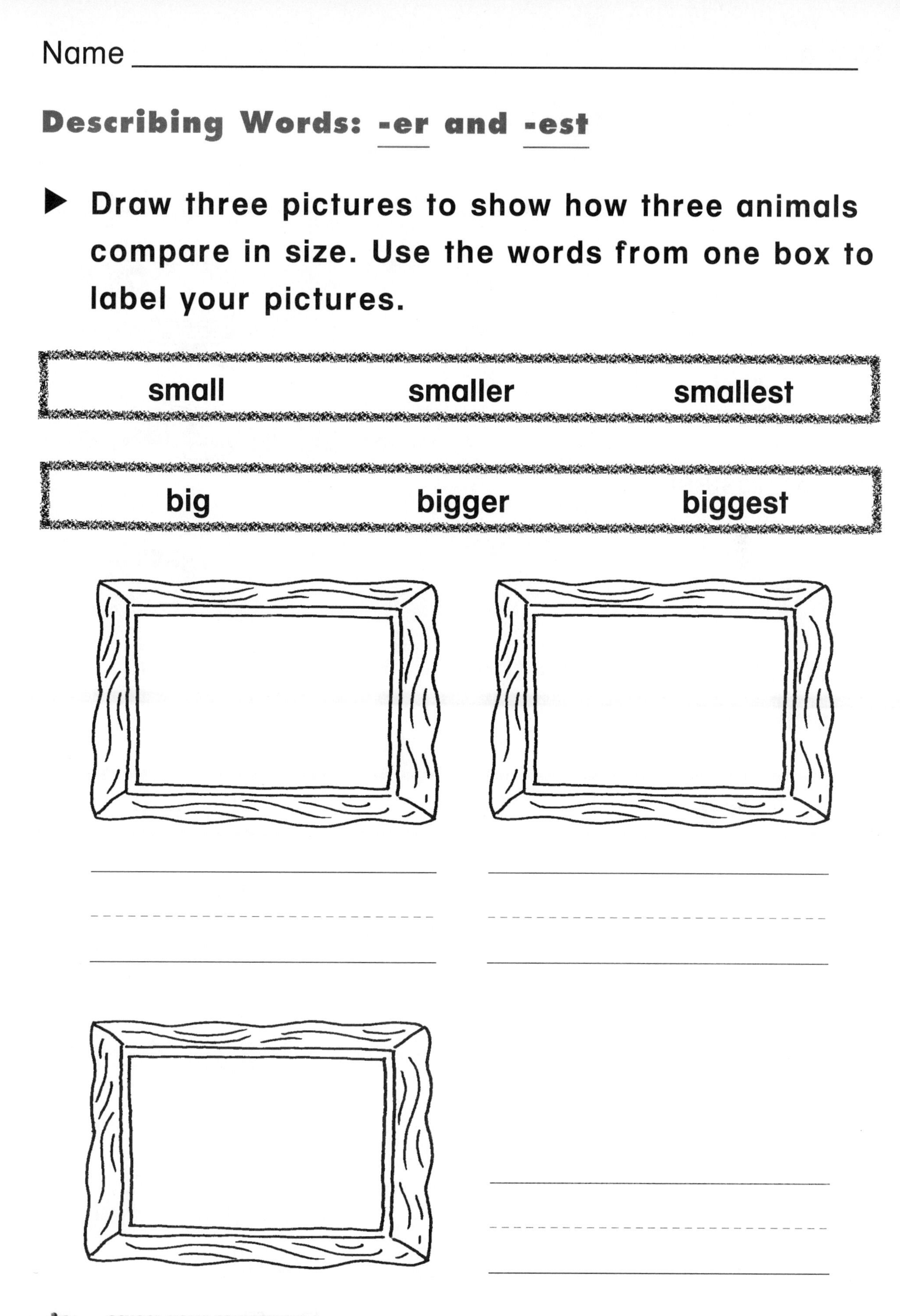

SCHOOL-HOME CONNECTION
Ask your child to say a sentence about each picture.

Name ______________________________

Describing Words: -er and -est

▶ **Draw a line from the word to the correct picture.**

1. fast
2. faster
3. fastest

▶ **Write a word from the box to complete each sentence.**

long	longer	longest

1. The cart is ______________.
2. The bus is ______________.
3. The train is the ______________ of all.

SCHOOL-HOME CONNECTION
Ask your child to use the words *slow, slower,* and *slowest* in sentences.

Name ______________________

Describing Words: -er and -est

▶ **Circle the word that completes each sentence about the picture. Then write the word.**

smaller smallest

1. The hen is ______________ than the pig.

smaller smallest

2. The pig is ______________ than the horse.

tallest taller

3. The horse is the ______________ of all.

smaller smallest

4. The bird is the ______________ of all.

SCHOOL-HOME CONNECTION
Ask your child to use the following words in sentences about herself or himself: *happy, happier, happiest.*

Name ______________________________

Verbs

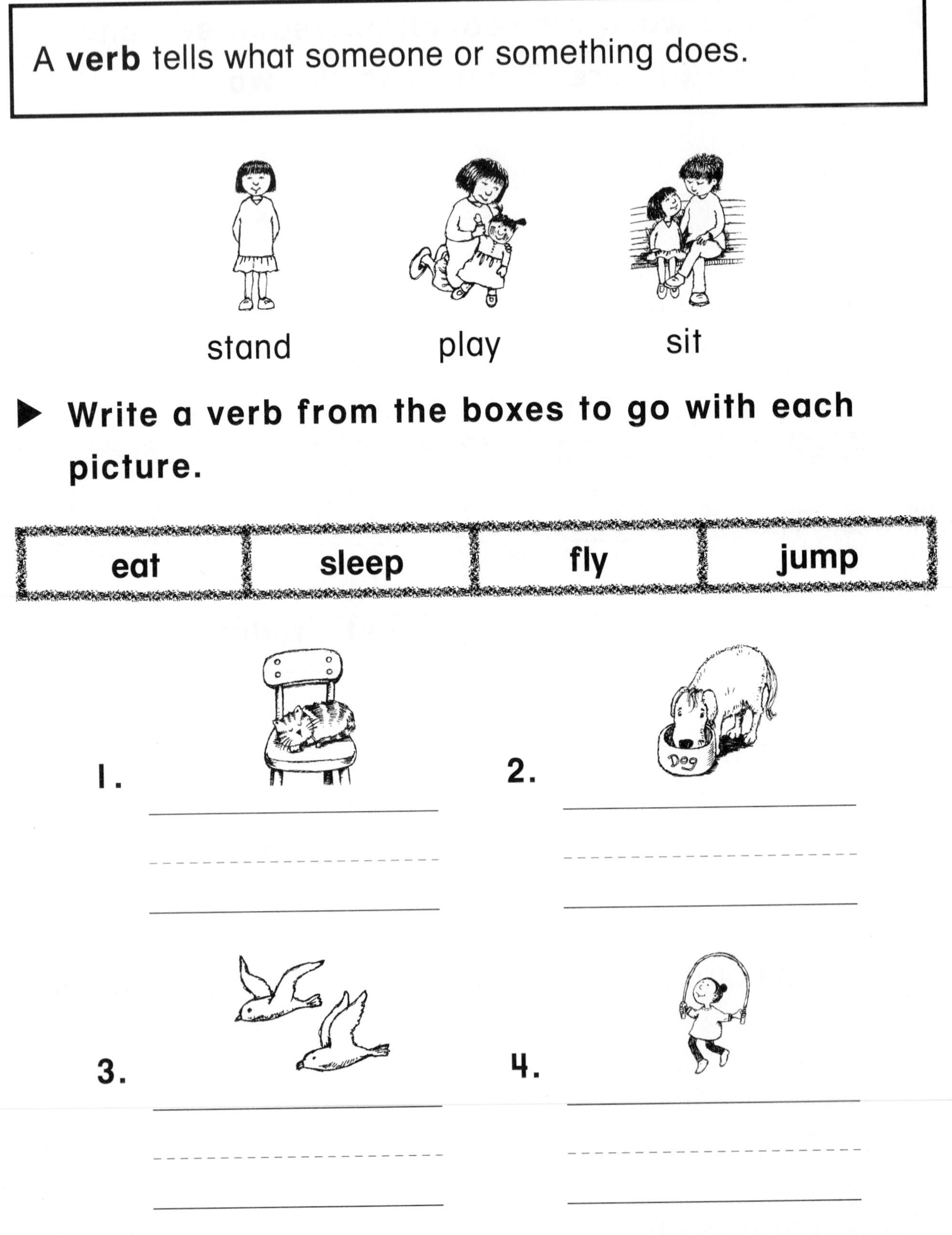

A **verb** tells what someone or something does.

stand play sit

▶ **Write a verb from the boxes to go with each picture.**

eat	sleep	fly	jump

1. ____________

2. ____________

3. ____________

4. ____________

SCHOOL-HOME CONNECTION
Have your child use the verbs in sentences about the pictures.

Name ______________________________

Verbs

▶ **Circle and then write each verb.**

1. hop frogs

2. children play

3. ducks fly

4. mother shouts

5. sleeps dog

SCHOOL-HOME CONNECTION
Ask your child to name some verbs that tell what children can do.

Name ______________________________

Verbs

▶ **Circle the verb in each sentence. Then write the word.**

1. We climb the hill. ____________

2. We hike on a path. ____________

3. Our dog runs up the hill, too.

____

4. We rest at the top.

____

5. We eat our fruit and cake.

____

SCHOOL-HOME CONNECTION
Ask your child to name some verbs that tell what she or he did at school today.

Name ________________________________

Verbs

▶ **Write the verb that completes each sentence. Use the words in the boxes.**

hatch	plays	sleeps
walks	eats	

1. The chicks ______________ from their eggs.

2. Mandy ______________ with her dog.

3. Her dad ______________ home.

4. The cat ______________ on the rug.

5. Her brother ______________ a snack.

SCHOOL-HOME CONNECTION
Ask your child to tell a different telling part for each sentence.

Name ______________________________

Verbs That Tell About Now

A **verb** can tell about **now**.

An s is added to some verbs that tell about now. The s is added when the verb tells what one person, place, or thing does.

Many girls run now. One girl runs now.

▶ **Write the correct verb under each picture. Use the words in the boxes.**

waves	runs	sit	kicks

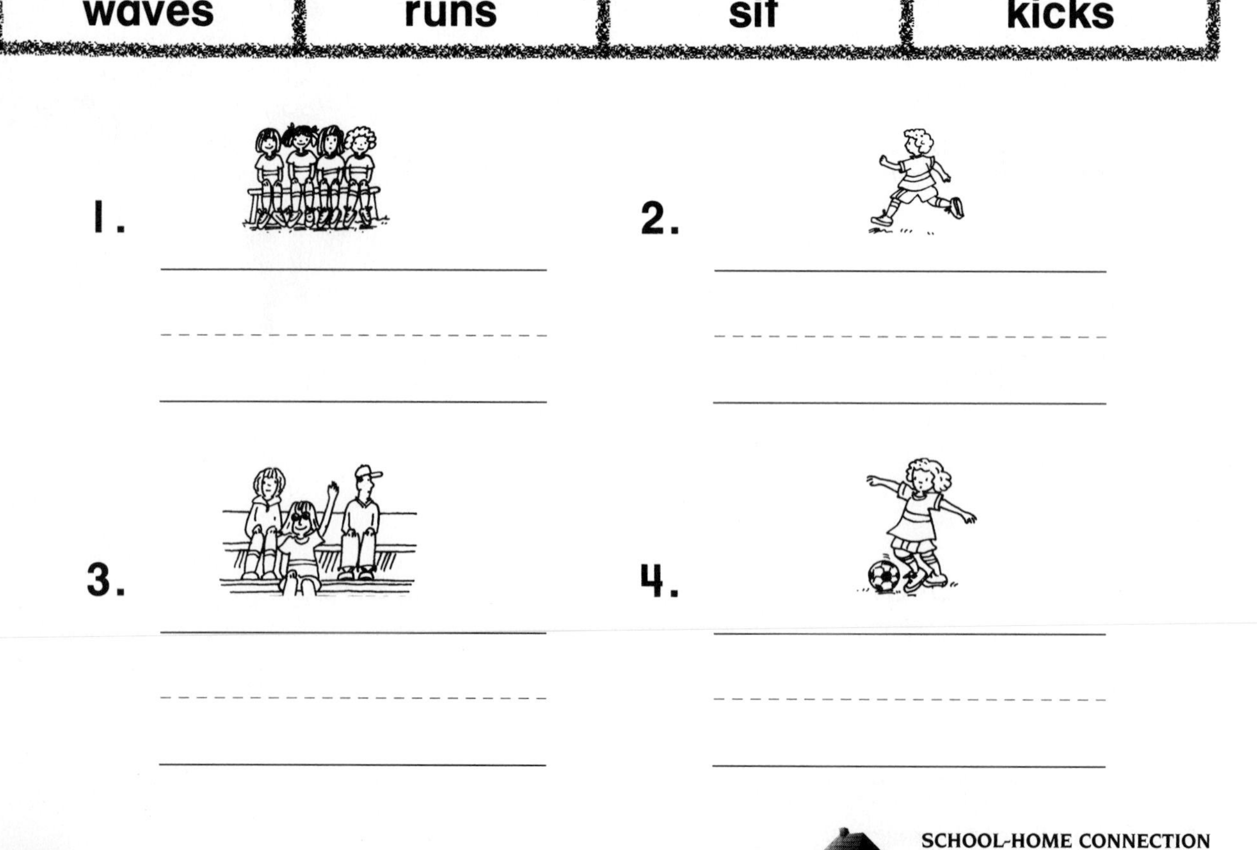

1. ______________________

2. ______________________

3. ______________________

4. ______________________

SCHOOL-HOME CONNECTION

Name ___________________________

Verbs That Tell About Now

▶ **Underline the naming part of each sentence. Then write the verbs that tell about now.**

1. The ducks fly by.

2. Children slide on the slope.

3. Marta makes a silly face.

4. Carlos claps his hands.

5. Mom and Dad sit on the bench.

SCHOOL-HOME CONNECTION
Ask your child to tell a different telling part for each sentence.

Name ____________________

Verbs That Tell About Now

▶ **Add s to each verb. Write the word in the sentence.**

stand

1. A man ____________________.

run

2. A horse ____________________.

dance

3. A dog ____________________.

clap

4. A little girl ____________________.

SCHOOL-HOME CONNECTION

Name ______________________________

Verbs That Tell About Now

▶ **Circle and write the correct verb.**

meet meets

1. The children ______________ at Mike's house.

bring brings

2. Jane ______________ a snack.

walk walks

3. They ______________ to the park.

sees see

4. Joey ______________ a friend.

makes make

5. The children ______________ a kite.

SCHOOL-HOME CONNECTION
Ask your child to tell a different telling part for each sentence.

Name ______________________________

Using Am, Is, and Are

The words **am**, **is**, and **are** tell about now.

Use **am** to tell about yourself.

Use **is** to tell about one person, place, or thing.

Use **are** to tell about more than one person, place, or thing.

I am happy.

Mom is busy.

Pets are fun.

▶ **Write am, is, or are to complete each sentence.**

1. I ______________ a girl named Molly.

2. My mother ______________ a vet.

3. Five animals ______________ in our home now.

SCHOOL-HOME CONNECTION

Name ____________________

Using Am, Is, and Are

▶ **Circle the words that complete the sentence. Color the picture the sentence tells about.**

1. The pigs **are pink.** / **is pink.**

2. The dog **is hungry.** / **are hungry.**

3. The elephants **is big.** / **are big.**

4. I **am happy.** / **is happy.**

▶ **Use is or are to complete the sentence.**

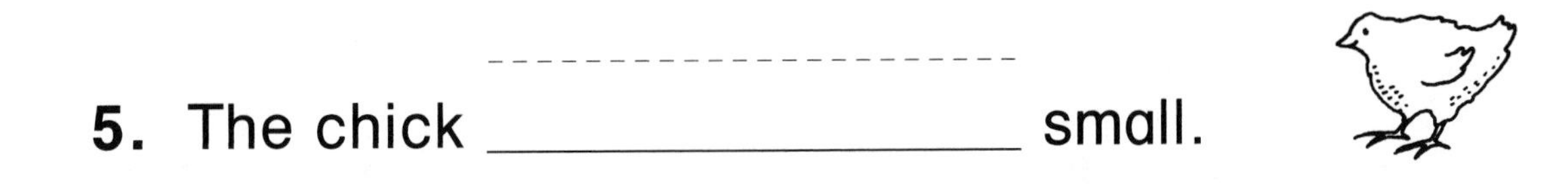

5. The chick ____________ small.

SCHOOL-HOME CONNECTION
Ask your child to tell a different telling part for each sentence.

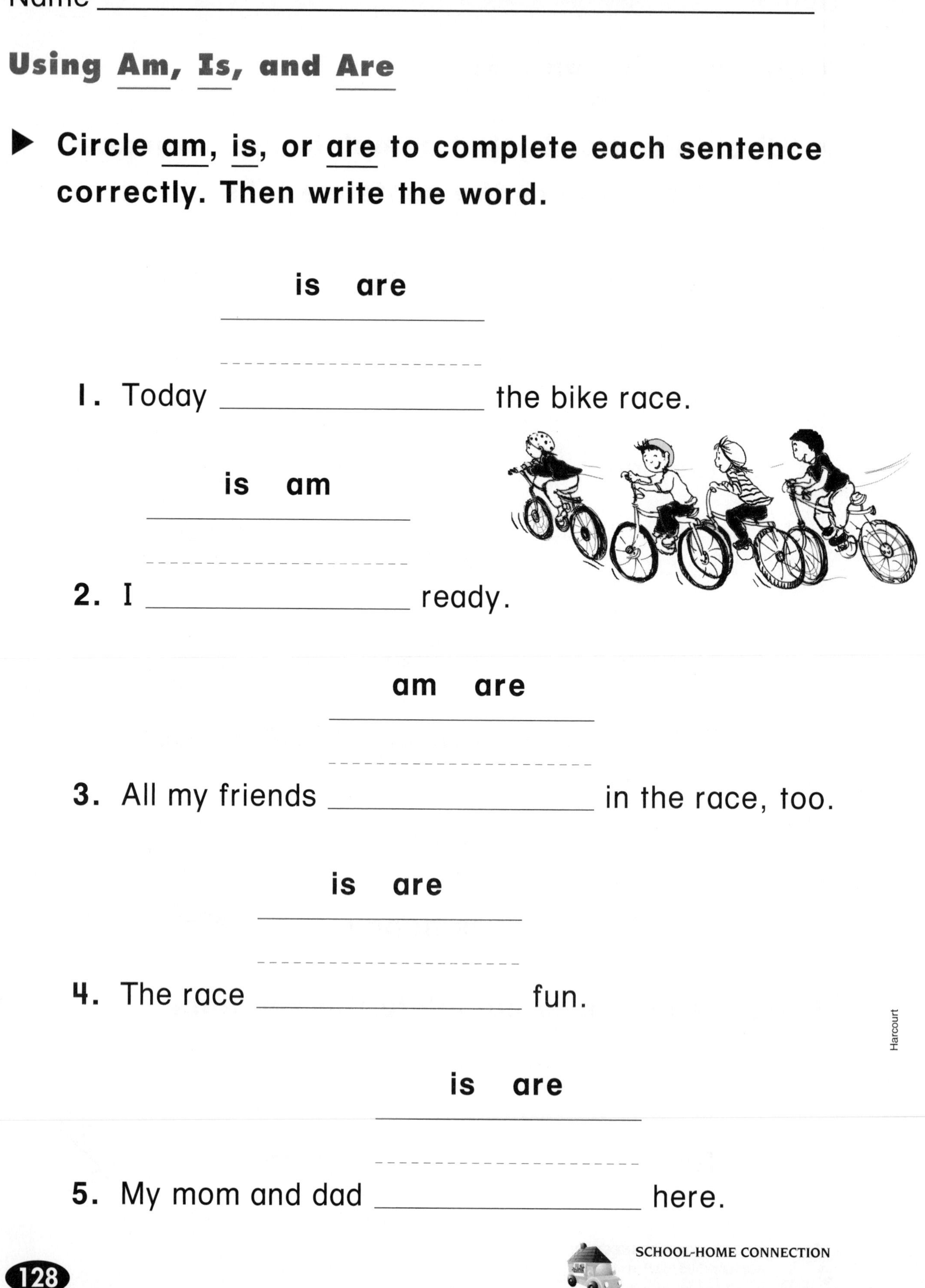

Name ______________________________

Using Am, Is, and Are

▶ **Circle am, is, or are to complete each sentence correctly. Then write the word.**

is are

1. Today ______________ the bike race.

is am

2. I ______________ ready.

am are

3. All my friends ______________ in the race, too.

is are

4. The race ______________ fun.

is are

5. My mom and dad ______________ here.

SCHOOL-HOME CONNECTION

Name ______________________________

Using Am, Is, and Are

▶ **Draw a line to complete each sentence. Then draw a picture to answer the riddle.**

What Am I?

1. I	is outside.
2. Some people	is the best weather for me.
3. My home	am a long animal.
4. Hot weather	are afraid of me.

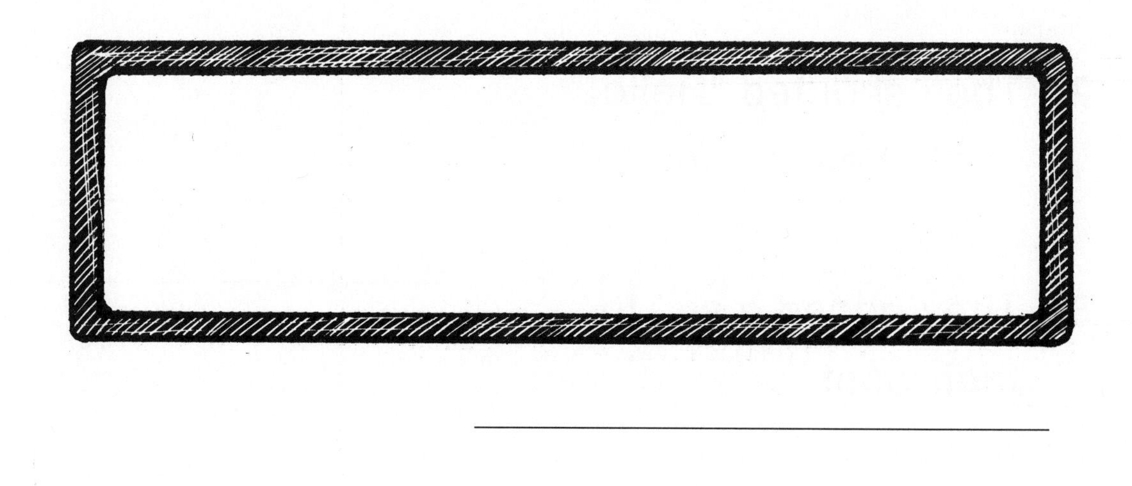

What am I? I am a ______________________.

snake

SCHOOL-HOME CONNECTION
Ask your child to tell a different telling part for each sentence.

Name ____________________

Verbs That Tell About the Past

A verb can tell about the **past**. Some verbs that tell about the past end with **ed**.

Two goats played in their boat.

They jumped into the water.

▶ **Write the verbs that tell about the past.**

1. The goats painted their boat green. ____________________

2. They shouted "Hello!" to all their friends. ____________________

3. They added a sail to their boat. ____________________

4. They sailed their boat on the lake. ____________________

SCHOOL-HOME CONNECTION
Ask your child to say some sentences about what he or she did in school.

Name ______________________________

Verbs That Tell About the Past

▶ **Underline the verb that tells about the past.**

1.	fill	filled	**2.**	picked	pick
3.	shouted	shouts	**4.**	want	wanted
5.	jumped	jumping	**6.**	roll	rolled
7.	walk	walked	**8.**	helped	help

▶ **Change each verb to tell about the past.**

9. look ______________________________

10. dance ______________________________

11. paint ______________________________

12. chirp ______________________________

SCHOOL-HOME CONNECTION
Have your child use the written words in sentences.

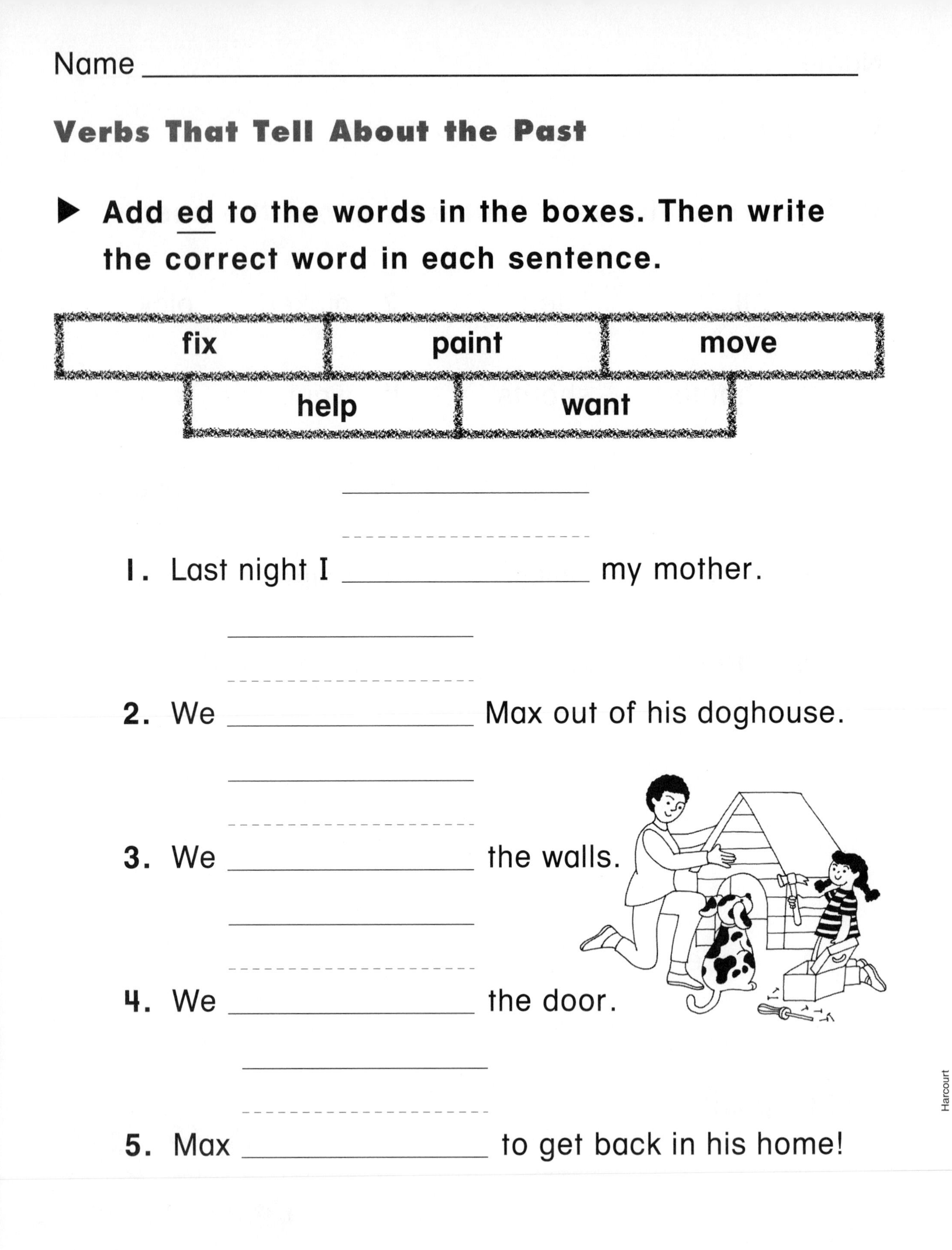

Name ____________________

Verbs That Tell About the Past

▶ **Add ed to the words in the boxes. Then write the correct word in each sentence.**

fix	paint	move
help	want	

1. Last night I ________ my mother.

2. We ________ Max out of his doghouse.

3. We ________ the walls.

4. We ________ the door.

5. Max ________ to get back in his home!

SCHOOL-HOME CONNECTION
Ask your child to tell about something you did together in the past.

Name ___

Verbs That Tell About the Past

▶ **Write the verbs that tell about the past.**

chirp chirped

1. The birds ___ all night.

jumped jump

2. The dog ___ on the bed.

splash splashed

3. The fish ___ their water.

played play

4. The cat ___ with her toys.

toss tossed

5. Carmen ___ in her bed!

SCHOOL-HOME CONNECTION Ask your child to tell about things that happened last night.

Name ______________________________

Using <u>Was</u> and <u>Were</u>

The words **was** and **were** tell about the past.

Use **was** to tell about one person, place, or thing.

Use **were** to tell about more than one person, place, or thing.

Our class play was funny.

The animals were silly.

▶ **Write was or were to complete each sentence.**

1. Dan ______________ a caterpillar.

2. Some children ______________ pigs.

3. Polly ______________ a whale.

4. The songs ______________ nice.

SCHOOL-HOME CONNECTION
Have your child use *was* and *were* in some sentences.

Name ______________________________

Using <u>Was</u> and <u>Were</u>

▶ **Draw a line to complete each sentence.**

1. The bus	were red and pink.
2. The trip	was big and yellow.
3. The flowers	were hungry.
4. The animals	was very tall.
5. The horse	was fun.

▶ **Write <u>was</u> or <u>were</u> to complete the sentence.**

The children ______________ happy.

Harcourt

SCHOOL-HOME CONNECTION
Have your child use *was* and *were* in sentences with these words: *I, we, cats, school.*

Name ______________________________

Using Was and Were

▶ **Circle was or were to complete each sentence. Write the sentence.**

1. The party ___ fun. **was** **were**

2. The hats ___ silly. **was** **were**

3. Dad ___ busy. **was** **were**

4. The cake ___ yummy. **was** **were**

▶ **Draw a picture about a party you went to.**

SCHOOL-HOME CONNECTION Ask your child to use *was* and *were* to tell about his or her picture.

Name ____________________

Using Was and Were

▶ **Write was or were to complete the sentences.**

Dear Gram,

Last night we went to a play.

The story __________ wonderful.

The people __________ funny.

It __________ a very long play.

We __________ all tired!

Love,

Lilly

Harcourt

SCHOOL-HOME CONNECTION
Help your child write a letter to a family member. Use *was* and *were*.

Name ______________________________

Using Go and Went

The word **go** tells about now.

The word **went** tells about the past.

We go to the country.

They went to the country the other day.

▶ **Write go or went to complete the story.**

1. Last week we ______________ to a farm.

2. The ducks ______________ into the water.

3. The sheep ______________ into the barn.

4. Today I ______________ to the mountains.

SCHOOL-HOME CONNECTION
Ask your child to use *go* and *went* in sentences.

Name ____________________

Using Go and Went

▶ **Write go or went in each sentence. Color the bus or car red if it tells about now. Color the bus or car green if it tells about the past.**

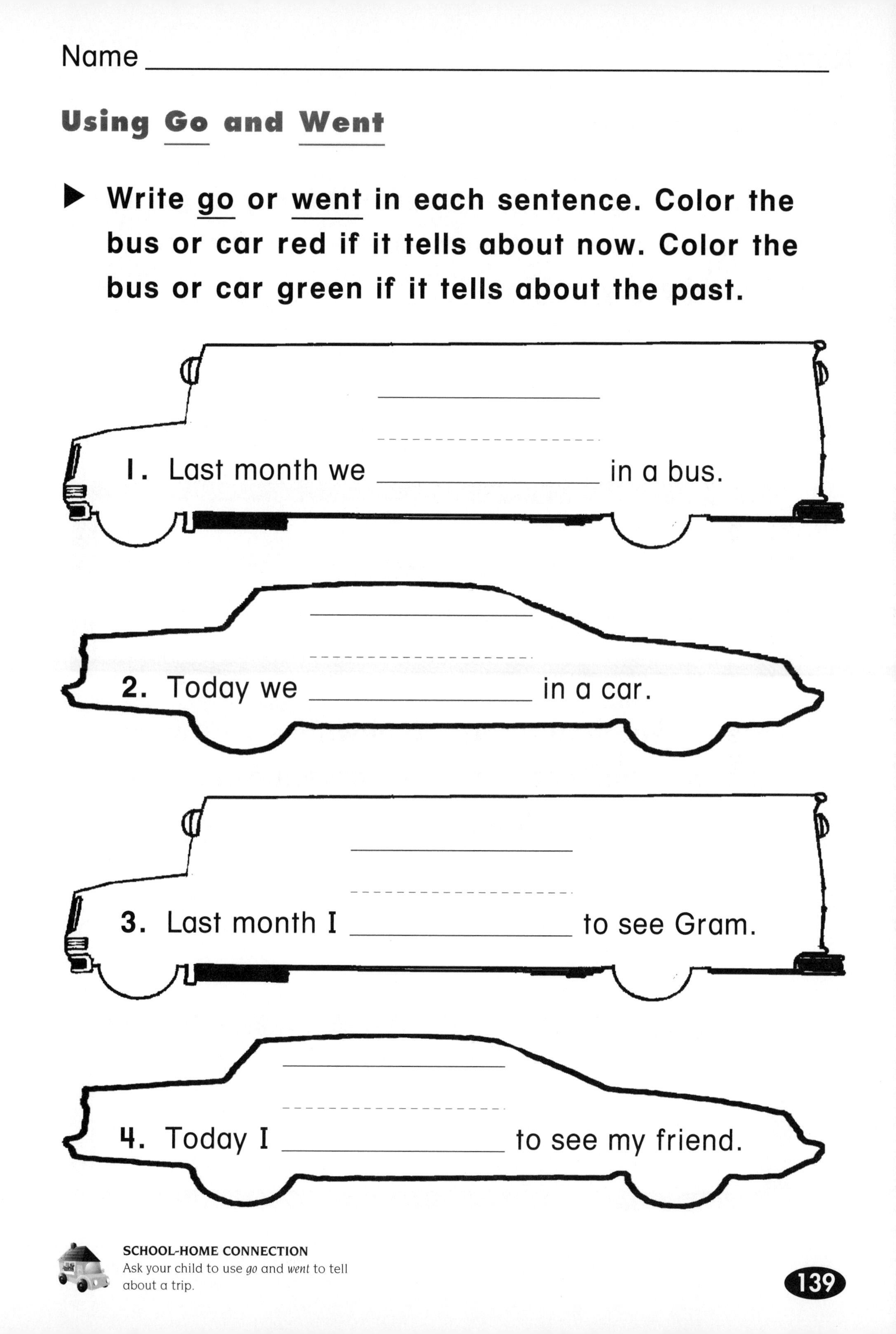

1. Last month we ____________ in a bus.

2. Today we ____________ in a car.

3. Last month I ____________ to see Gram.

4. Today I ____________ to see my friend.

SCHOOL-HOME CONNECTION
Ask your child to use *go* and *went* to tell about a trip.

Name ____________________

Using Go and Went

▶ Write a sentence about somewhere you go now. Use go in your sentence. Draw a picture to show where you go.

▶ Write a sentence about somewhere you went last year. Use went in your sentence. Draw a picture to show where you went.

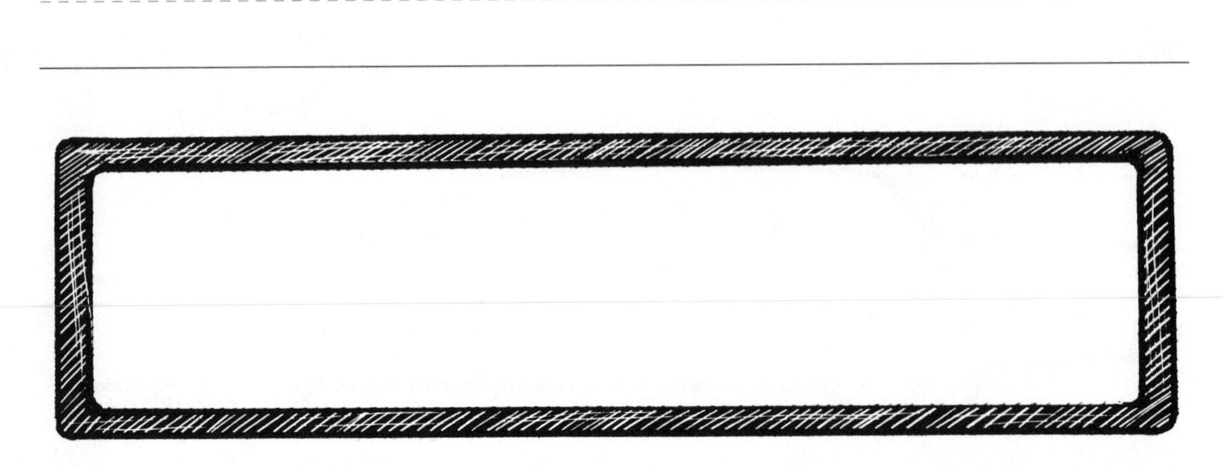

SCHOOL-HOME CONNECTION
Have your child use *go* and *went* to tell about the pictures.

Name ______________________________

Using Go and Went

▶ **Write go or went to complete the sentences. Make these sentences tell about now.**

1. Today Dad and I ______________ on a hike.

2. We ______________ to the mountains.

▶ **Make these sentences tell about the past.**

3. Last month Mom and I ______________ to the beach.

4. We ______________ in the water.

SCHOOL-HOME CONNECTION
Ask your child to use *go* or *went* in another sentence about each picture.

Name ______________________________

Contractions with Not

There is a short way to write words with **not**. An apostrophe (') shows where letters are left out.

is + not = isn't	do + not = don't
did + not = didn't	will + not = won't

▶ **Circle and write the word that completes the sentence.**

wasn't didn't

1. Bill ___ know what the loud sound was. ______________

isn't won't

2. Now he ___ turn on the light. ______________

isn't don't

3. Bill ___ afraid of the dark. ______________

hasn't don't

4. He ___ called his mom or dad. ______________

SCHOOL-HOME CONNECTION
As your child reads the sentences, ask him or her to say the two words that form the contractions.

Name ____________________

Contractions with Not

▶ **Read each sentence. Write the contraction for the underlined words.**

isn't	wasn't	don't
aren't	weren't	didn't
hasn't	haven't	won't

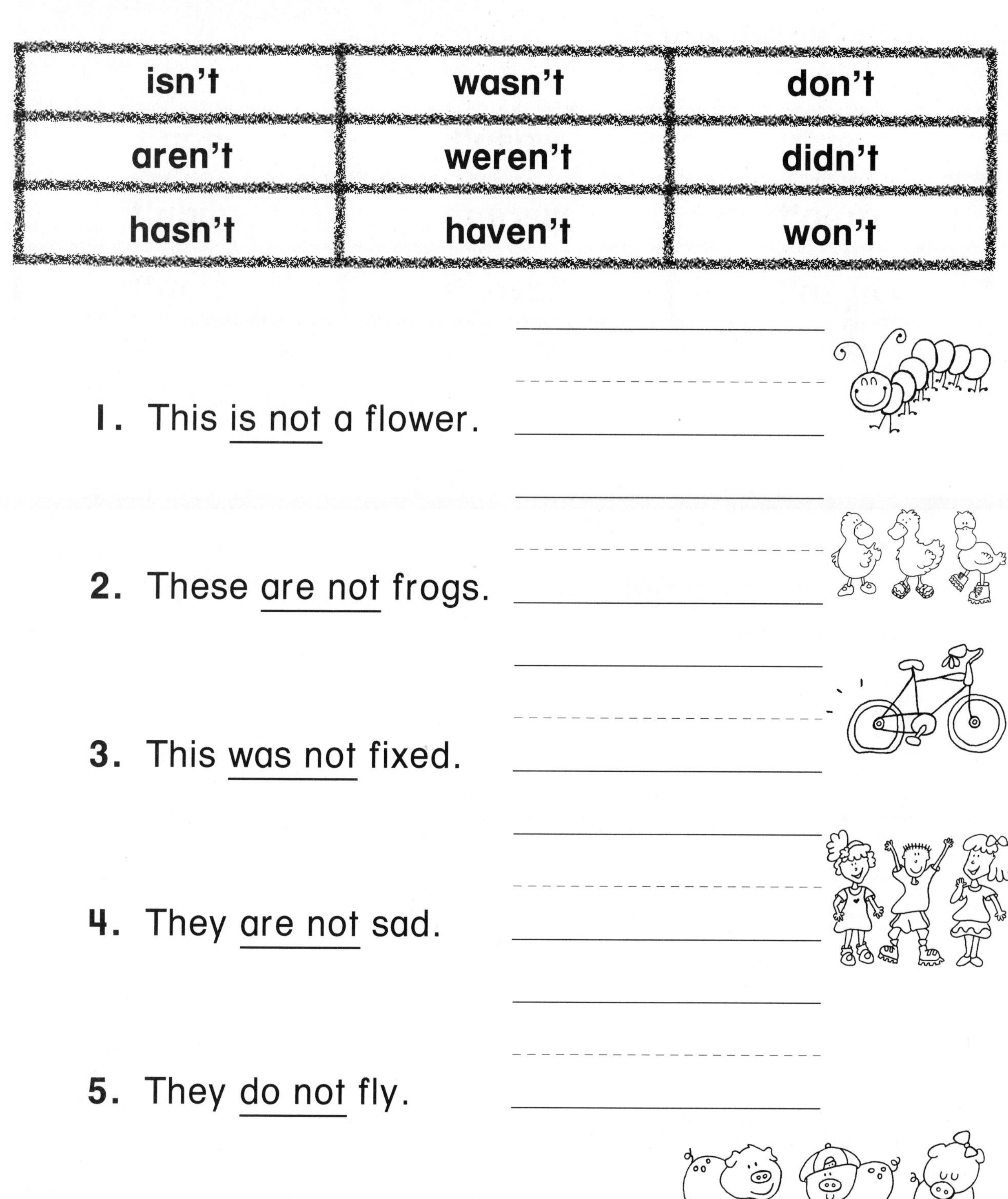

1. This is not a flower. ____________

2. These are not frogs. ____________

3. This was not fixed. ____________

4. They are not sad. ____________

5. They do not fly. ____________

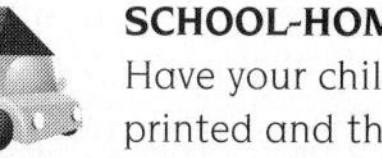

SCHOOL-HOME CONNECTION
Have your child read each sentence as printed and then with the contraction.

Name ______________________________

Contractions with Not

▶ **Read each sentence. Write the contraction for the underlined words.**

isn't	**wasn't**	**don't**
aren't	**weren't**	**didn't**
hasn't	**haven't**	**won't**

1. Many people are not ready. ______________

2. They have not put away their things. ______________

3. The train will not go yet. ______________

4. The alarm has not buzzed yet. ______________

5. We were not late! ______________

SCHOOL-HOME CONNECTION
Have your child read each sentence as printed and then with the contraction.

Name ______________________________

Contractions with Not

▶ **Match each pair of words with its contraction.**

isn't	wasn't	don't
aren't	weren't	didn't
hasn't	haven't	won't

1. is not	aren't
2. have not	don't
3. will not	wasn't
4. was not	isn't
5. do not	haven't
6. are not	won't
7. can not	wouldn't
8. would not	can't

SCHOOL-HOME CONNECTION
Ask your child to read the contractions in the boxes and tell what two words form them.

Handwriting

Handwriting

Capital and Lowercase Manuscript Alphabet

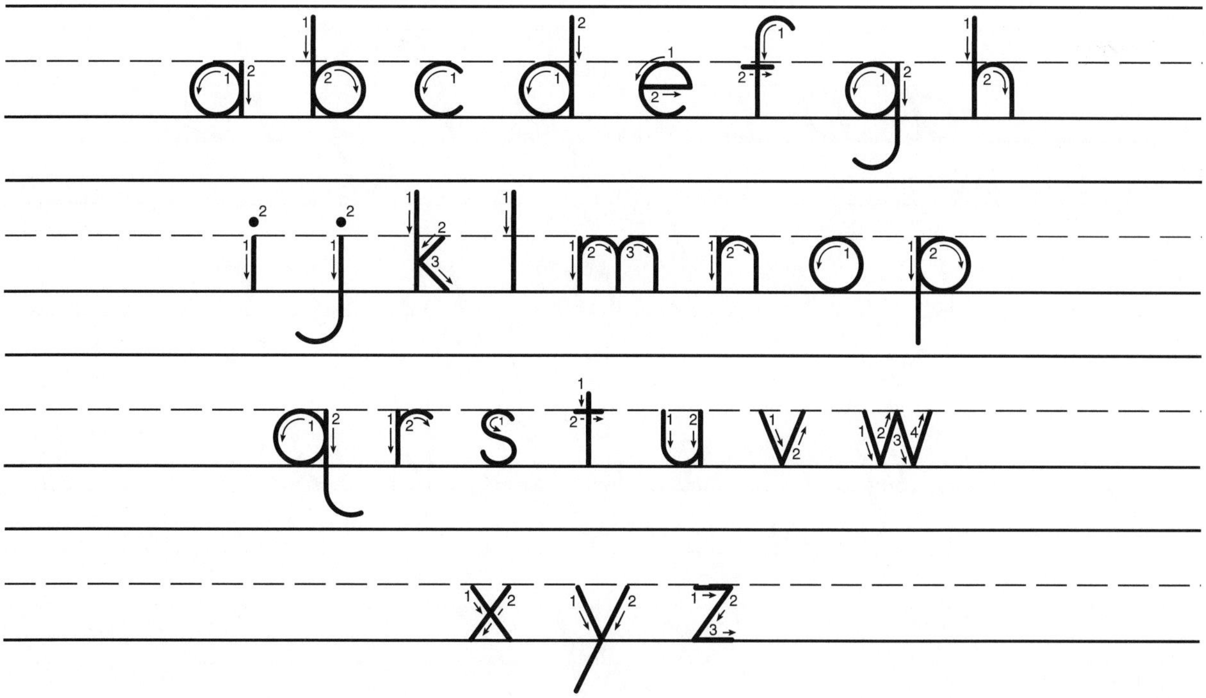

A B C D E F G H
I J K L M N O P
Q R S T U V W
X Y Z

a b c d e f g h
i j k l m n o p
q r s t u v w
x y z

Harcourt

Handwriting

D'Nealian Capital and Lowercase Alphabet

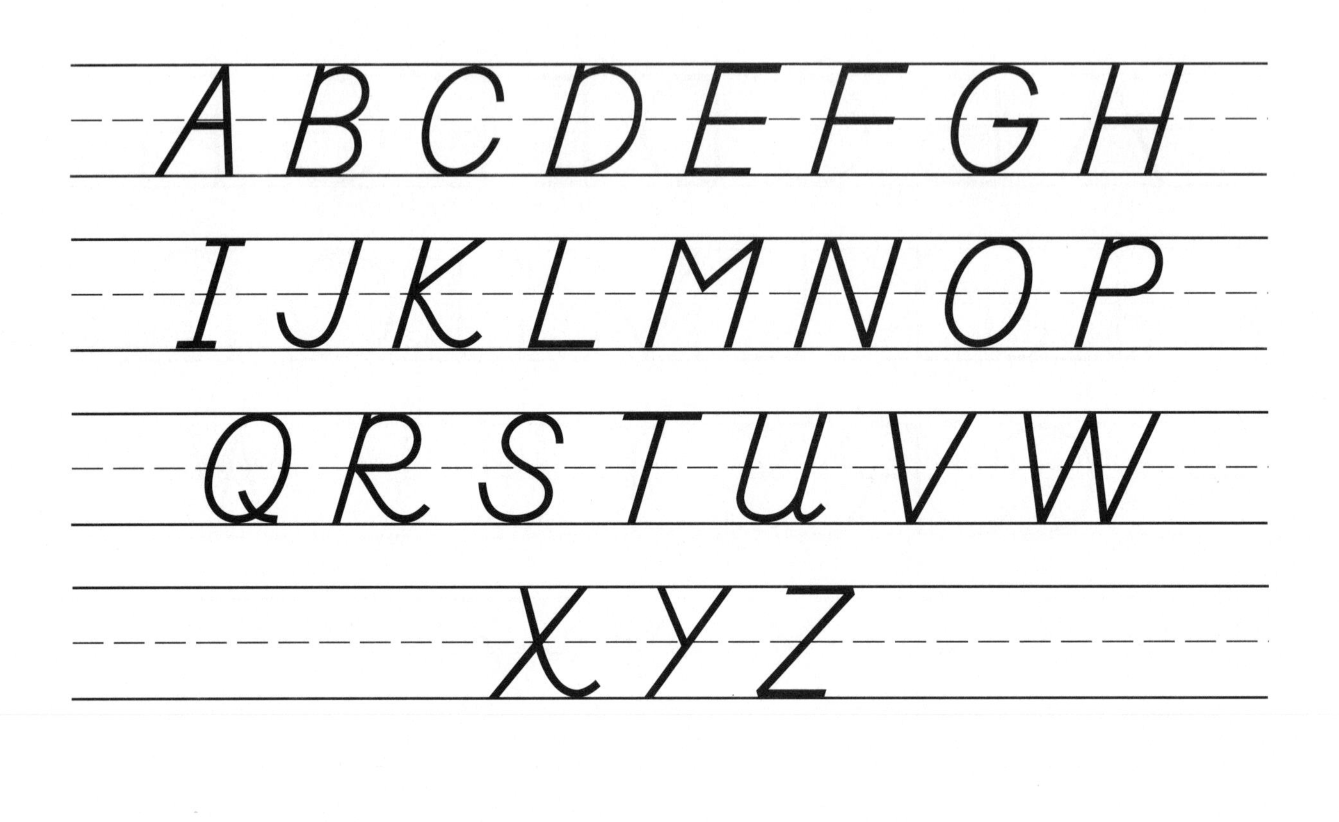

a b c d e f g h

i j k l m n o p

q r s t u v w

x y z

Elements of Handwriting

▶ **Be sure the letters you write are not too close together or too far apart.**

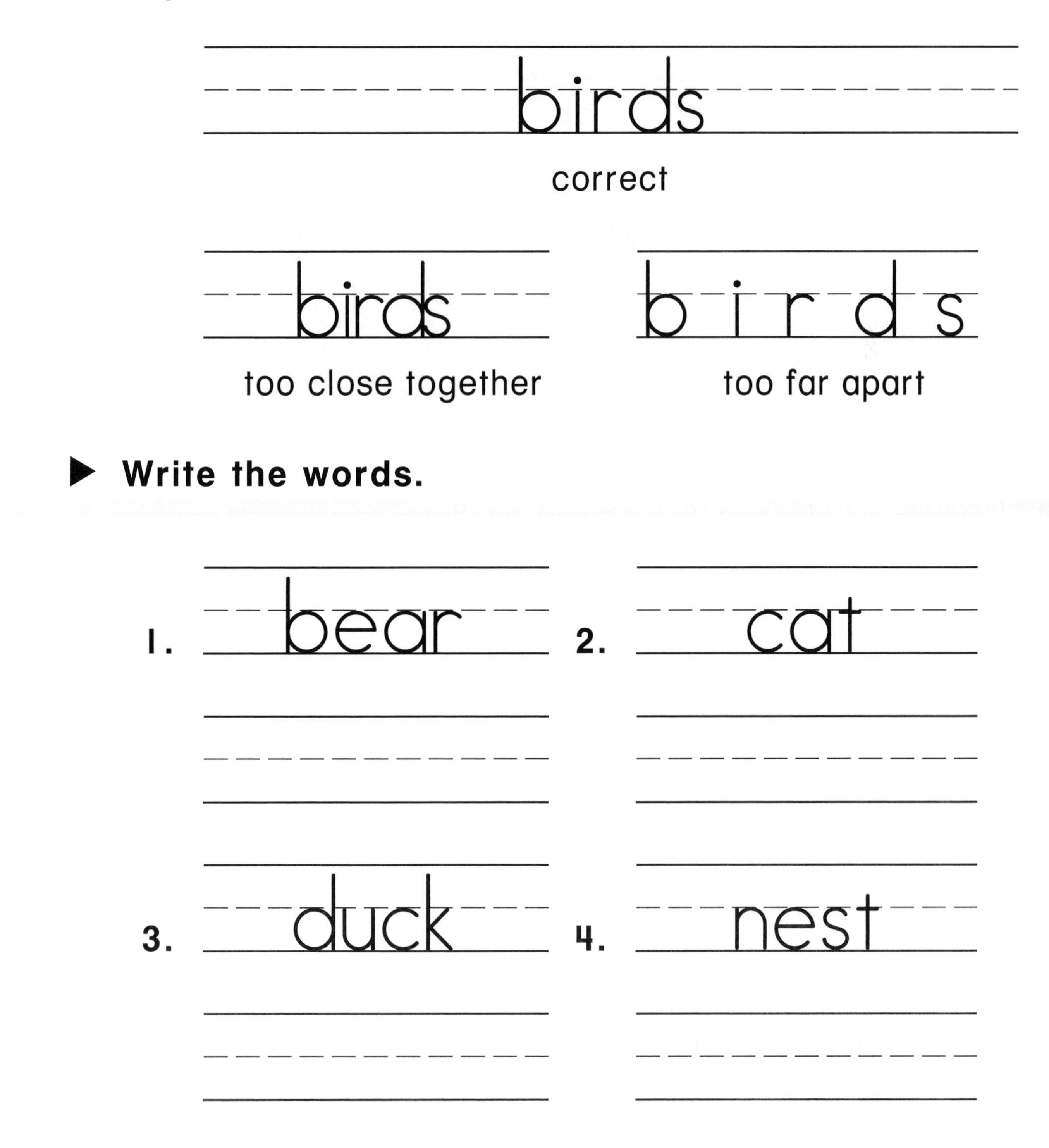

Harcourt

Elements of Handwriting

▶ **Be sure the spacing between words is correct.**

incorrect spacing

correct spacing

▶ **Write the sentences.**

1. Today is sunny.

2. Summer is fun.

3. You can swim.

Common Errors—Manuscript Letters

▶ **Write the letters correctly.**

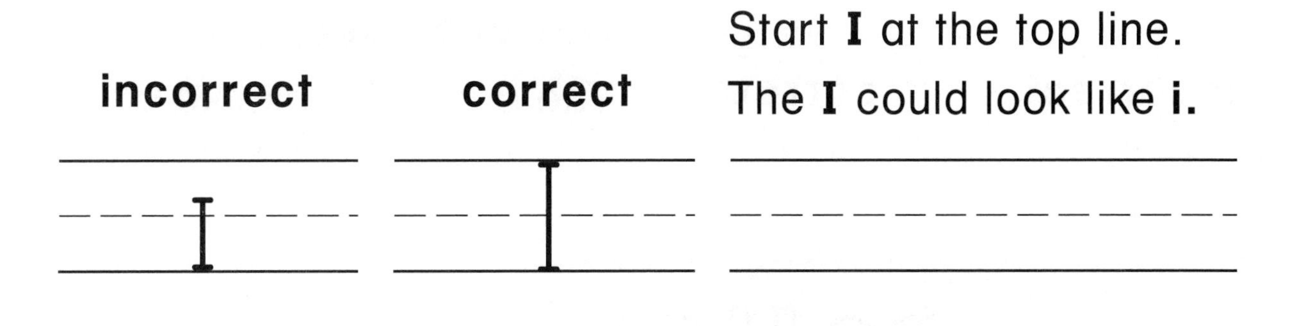

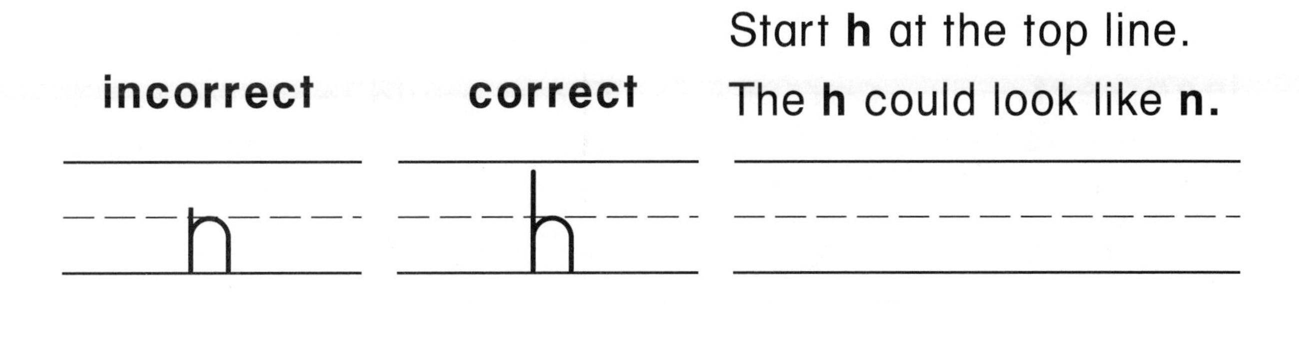

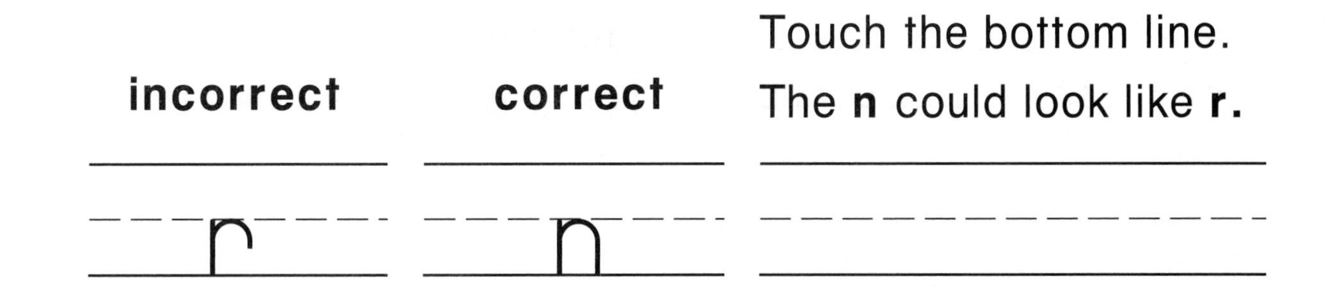

Common Errors—Manuscript Letters

▶ **Write the letters correctly.**

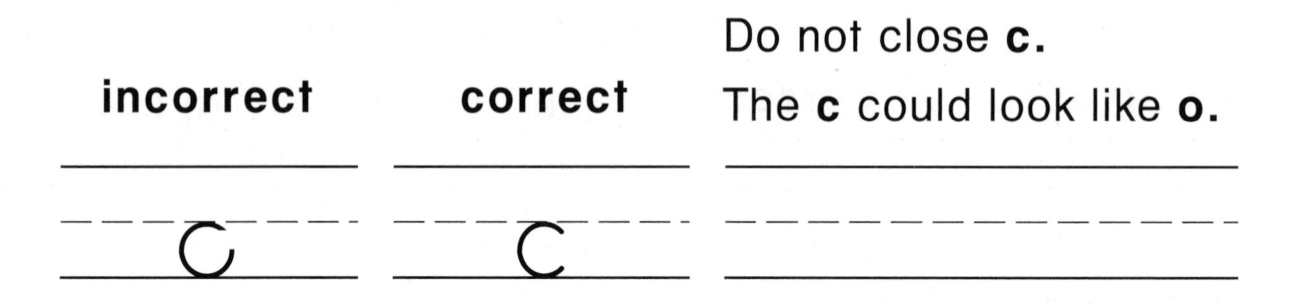

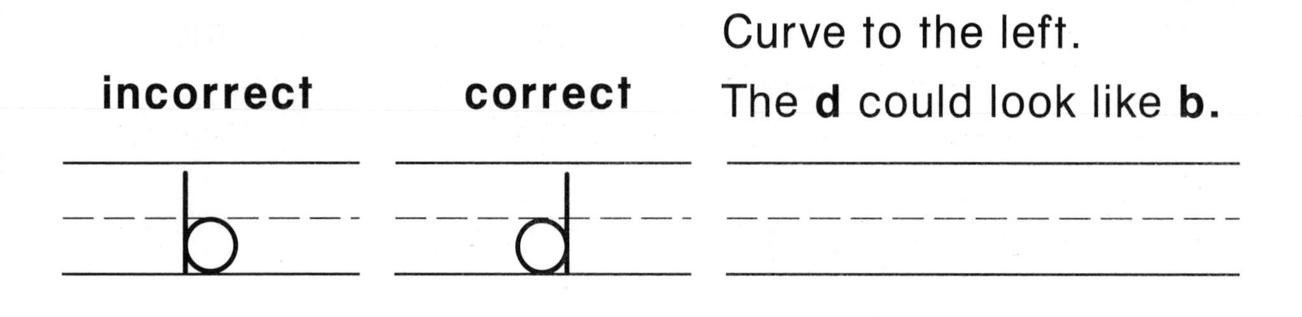

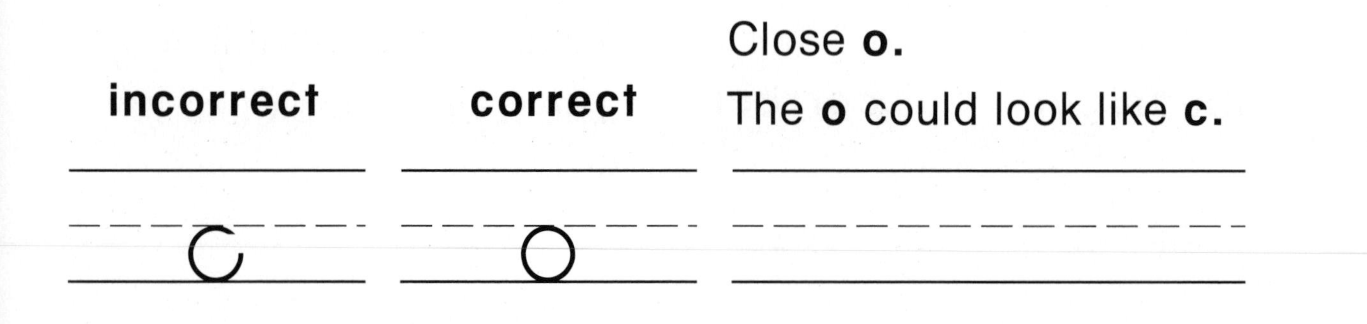

Common Errors—Manuscript Letters

▶ Write the letters correctly.

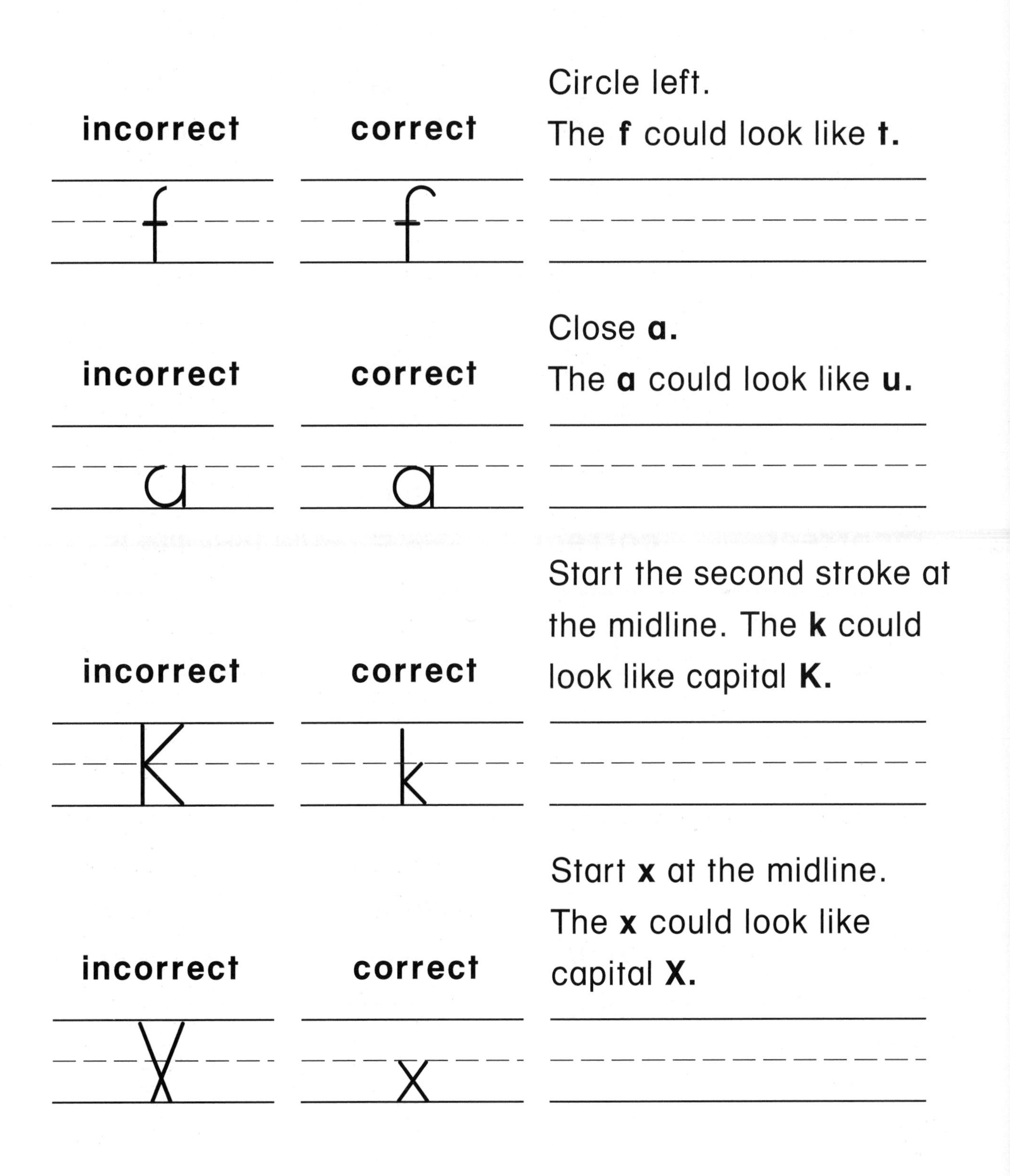

Circle left.
The **f** could look like **t.**

incorrect f correct f

Close **a.**
The **a** could look like **u.**

incorrect a correct a

Start the second stroke at the midline. The **k** could look like capital **K.**

incorrect K correct k

Start **x** at the midline. The **x** could look like capital **X.**

incorrect X correct x

Common Errors—Manuscript Letters

▶ **Write the letters correctly.**

Cross **T** at the top line.
The **T** could look like **t.**

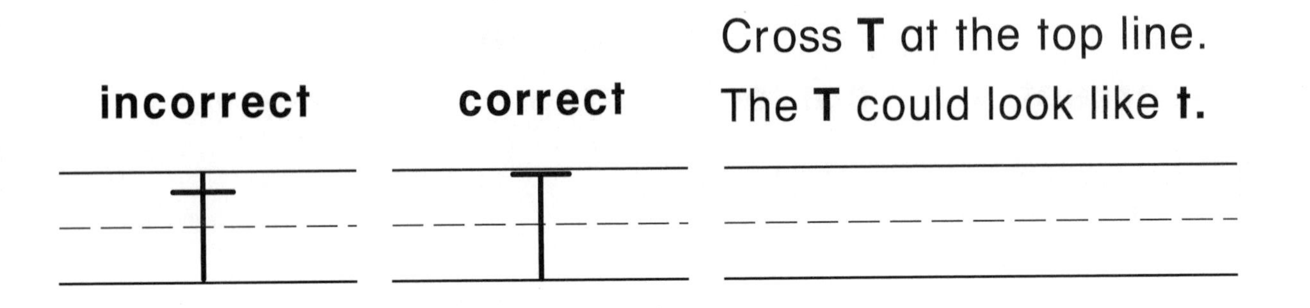

Use all the touchpoints.
The **E** could look like **F.**

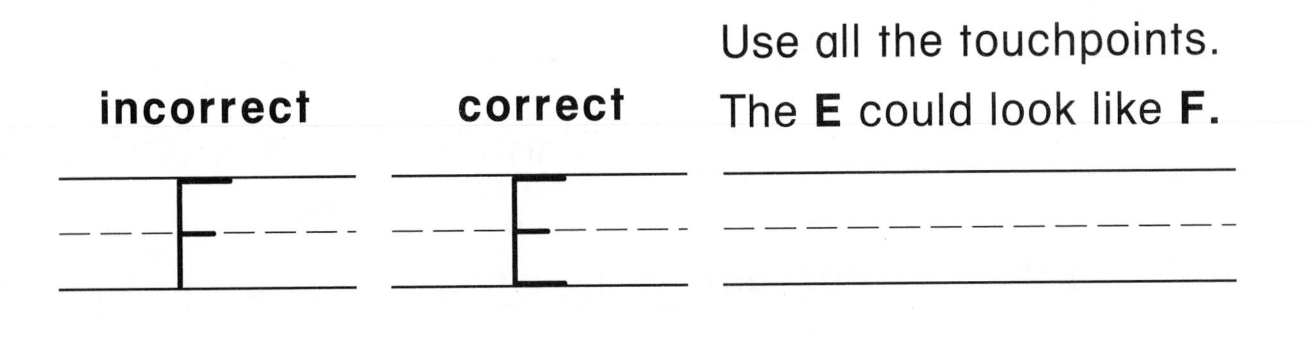

Use the short slant stroke.
The **Q** could look like **O.**

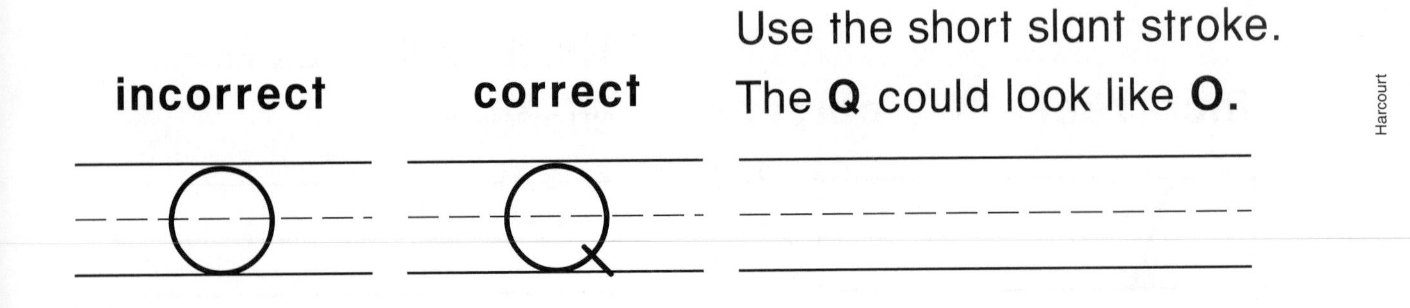

Common Errors—Manuscript Letters

▶ **Write the letters correctly.**

Use the straight-across stroke.
The **G** could look like **C.**

incorrect **correct**

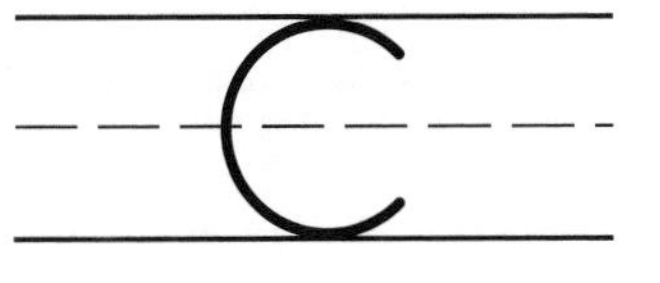

Make your strokes go straight up and down.
The **U** could look like **O.**

incorrect **correct**

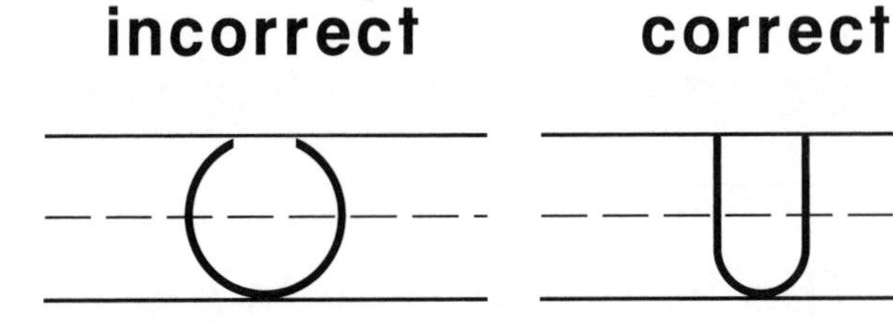

Do not curve the slant stroke.
The **R** could look like **B.**

incorrect **correct**

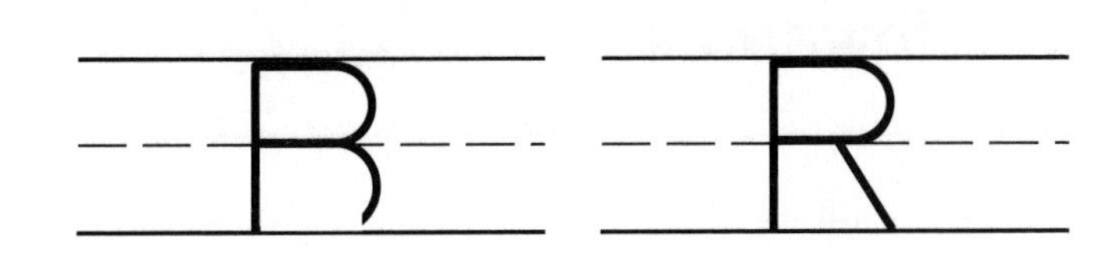

Common Errors—Manuscript Letters

▶ **Write the letters correctly.**

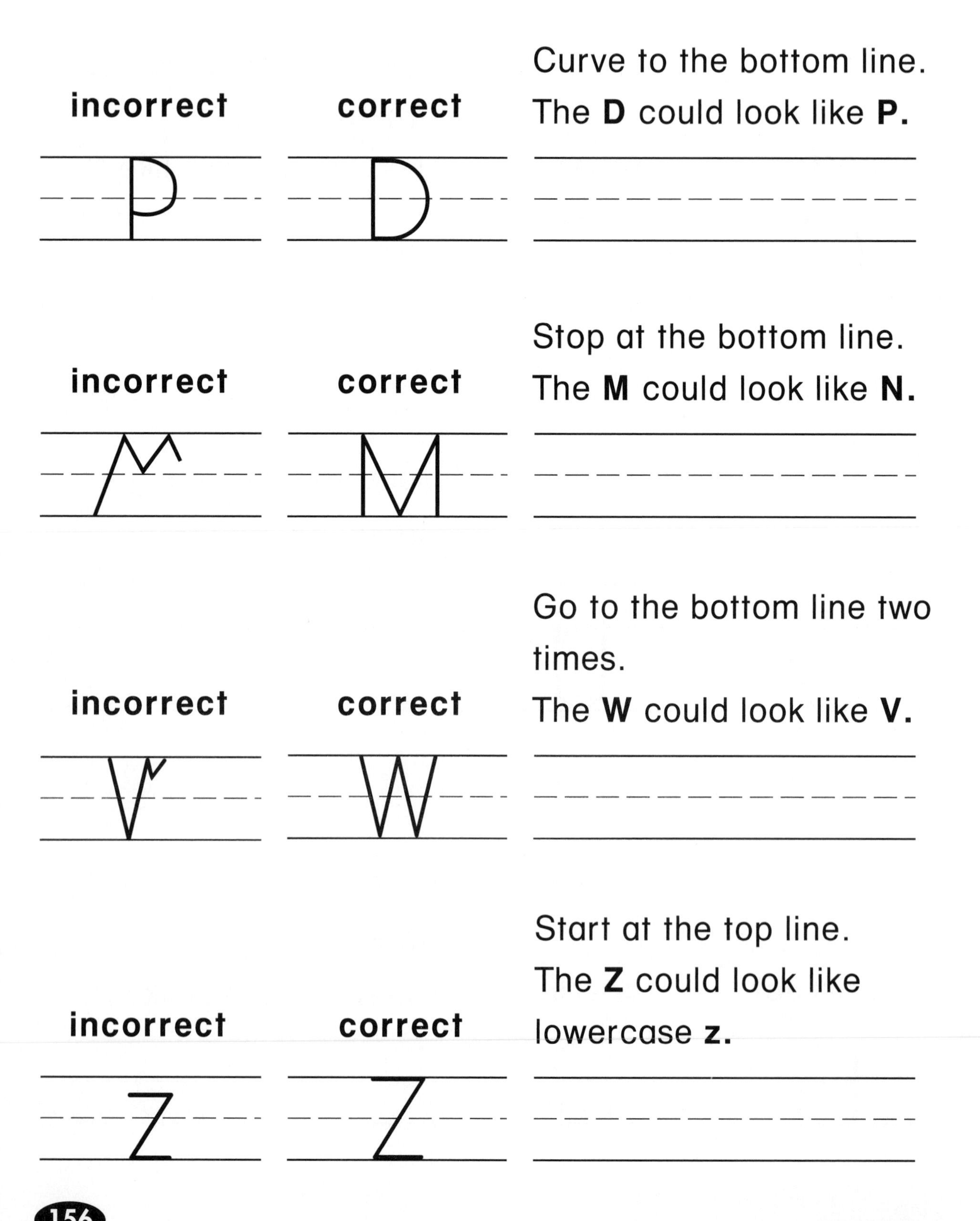

SCHOOL-HOME CONNECTION
Children can use this page when they draw a picture and write sentences about it. (See page 3.)

Name ______________________________

SCHOOL-HOME CONNECTION
Children can use this page when they write a story. (See pages 4 and 8.)

Name ______________________

SCHOOL-HOME CONNECTION
Children can use this page when they write a poem. (See page 5.)

Name

Harcourt

SCHOOL-HOME CONNECTION
Children can use this page when they write a friendly letter. (See page 6.)

Name

Title

Author

What is this book about?

What is your favorite part?

SCHOOL-HOME CONNECTION
Children can use this page when they write a book report. (See page 10.)